33 Days to the Holy Family

Consecration to Jesus, Mary, and Joseph

Donald H. Calloway, MIC

& Scott L. Smith, Jr.

Available from:
Marian Helpers Center, Stockbridge, MA 01263
Prayerline: 1-800-804-3823
Orderline: 1-800-462-7426

Websites:
FatherCalloway.org
Marian.org

Publication Date: January 1, 2026
Solemnity of Mary, Mother of God

Library of Congress Control Number: 2025947308
ISBN: 978-1-59614-660-0

Imprimi Potest:
Very Rev. Chris Alar, MIC, Provincial Superior
The Blessed Virgin Mary, Mother of Mercy Province
September 23, 2025
Feast of St. Pius of Pietrelcina (Padre Pio)

Nihil Obstat:
Robert A. Stackpole, STD, Censor Deputatus
September 23, 2025

Note: The *Nihil Obstat* and corresponding *Imprimi Potest* are not a certification that those granting it agree with the contents, opinions, or statements expressed in the work. Instead, they merely confirm that the work contains nothing contrary to faith and morals.

Cover art: The Holy Family (1899) by Giuseppe Calì (1846-1930).
St. George's Basilica/Daniel Cilia. Gozo, Malta. Used with permission.

Table of Contents

Introduction

Did you find out about *33 Days to the Holy Family* and think to yourself, "Really? Another 33 Day consecration book? Aren't there enough of these kinds of books already?" It's understandable if you think that way. Nobody can deny that in the last 10 years or so there have been a lot of 33 Day consecration books written about consecrations to Mary, God the Father, St. Joseph, the Eucharist, Divine Mercy, etc. It can be a little overwhelming sometimes.

Nonetheless, the times that we live in are so evil and so fraught with theological and spiritual confusion that consecration-style books have helped a lot of people experience spiritual renewal and grow in hope. These books have served as catechetical tools by offering straightforward answers and doctrinal clarity on topics that are often misunderstood. In confusing times such as ours, it's good to have clarity, doctrinal precision, and black-and-white answers.

You most likely would agree that there is a lot of confusion today regarding the family. No matter where you look, governments, organizations, and institutions are promoting new definitions of family and marriage, women and men. They can't all be right! Shouldn't there be a God-given blueprint for this stuff, models that we can look to in order to know what these things actually are?

The answer is yes. Catholicism has the blueprints! It's Jesus, Mary, and Joseph, the Holy Family.

The Holy Family serves as the pattern and model for marriage and family, demonstrating what these are, as well as the correct understanding of masculinity and fatherhood, femininity and motherhood, babies and children. God knew the great confusion and diabolical social messiness that would occur in modern times. For this reason, beginning in the mid-19th century, He began to pour out His Holy Spirit and inspire popes, priests, nuns, and laity to initiate new movements that would focus on the Holy Family.

Let us explain.

On December 8, 1870, Blessed Pope Pius IX proclaimed St. Joseph the Patron of the Universal Church. The fruit of highlighting St. Joseph was an increased interest in and devotion to the Holy Family. For example, after Pius IX the popes began to write and speak about the Holy Family in official documents of the Church, and every pope following him has done so. New movements, associations, confraternities, and religious communities were founded to spread devotion to the Holy Family. Pope Benedict XV said, "With the increase of devotion to St. Joseph among the faithful there will necessarily result an increase in their devotion toward the Holy Family of Nazareth, of which he was the august head."[1]

Prior to the 1870 proclamation declaring St. Joseph the Universal Patron of the Church, there really wasn't much emphasis on the Holy Family in Catholic teaching and devotion. Obviously, the Holy Family has always been praised by the Church, and certain saints and ecclesial figures throughout history were particularly devoted to the Holy Family. Yet the Church never really saw the need to delve into this mystery of the faith. This "neglect" was certainly not due to any ill will or lack of love. To the contrary, until modern times, every Christian intrinsically loved the Holy Family, knowing that this mystery was at the core of Christianity. None of that was in doubt. There was no threat to the Holy Family or family life in general. Even in difficult times filled with moral decay and theological confusion in the Church, neither the Holy Family nor the family in general was questioned, attacked, or re-defined. Everyone knew what the terms man, father, woman, mother, and child meant. Even pagans and delusional heretics didn't seek to deconstruct the family.

Sadly, that's not the case today.

Did you know that the last great Catholic basilica still under construction in the world today is dedicated to the Holy Family and had its beginnings immediately after St. Joseph was proclaimed Patron of the Universal Church in

1870? It's the *Sagrada Familia* (Holy Family) Basilica in Barcelona, Spain. Construction began on March 19, 1882, the Solemnity of St. Joseph; and the basilica is still under construction in our day. Interestingly, the basilica was originally intended to be dedicated to St. Joseph and, secondarily, to the Holy Family. Shortly after the proclamation declaring St. Joseph the Patron of the Universal Church, José Maria Bocabella, a devout Catholic from Barcelona with a particular zeal for promoting St. Joseph, made a pilgrimage to Italy. While there, he was inspired by a visit to the Holy House of Loreto (the family home of Jesus, Mary, and Joseph from Nazareth which was mystically transported to Italy in the 13th century by angels). When he returned to Spain, he initiated the construction of a neo-Gothic church dedicated to St. Joseph and his Holy Family. In light of the Church's new emphasis on St. Joseph, Bocabella envisioned a shrine in Barcelona that emphasized St. Joseph — similar to how the Holy House of Loreto highlights the Virgin Mary and is often simply referred to as Our Lady of Loreto. He knew that something special was happening in the Church regarding St. Joseph, and he wanted to highlight his importance and draw people to the Holy Family through him. It was a brilliant idea, and the Holy Spirit inspired it and used it as the foundation for a basilica dedicated to the Holy Family.

One year after construction began, Bocabella became overwhelmed by the project and felt the need to step away from it. That same year, the architect he had hired also decided to resign. At that point, only the crypt of the shrine was complete, a crypt entirely dedicated to St. Joseph. It's an absolutely beautiful neo-Gothic chapel with an altar dedicated to St. Joseph at the center. Providentially, the crypt would end up serving as the pillar and foundation for the larger basilica that would come to be built over it, one entirely dedicated to the Holy Family.

In 1883, the renowned architect Antoni Gaudi took over the project. Gaudi himself was a devout Catholic. (His cause for canonization is currently under way.) When Gaudi took over the project, he and others decided to continue construction but with an important change: The rest of the basilica would be focused on the Holy Family. One of the reasons for this was because a very holy nun in Barcelona was seeing to the construction of a shrine dedicated to St. Joseph at that time. The nun was Blessed Petra of St. Joseph (1845–1906). She was very devoted to St. Joseph and even had visions of him. To have two shrines dedicated to St. Joseph in the same town would be odd. The shrine that Blessed Petra constructed is known today as The Royal Sanctuary of St. Joseph of the Mountain and is one of the most beautiful — if not *the* most beautiful — shrines dedicated to St. Joseph in the world. Much smaller than *Sagrada Familia* Basilica, it's built in the Neo-Romanesque style and was completed in 1902.

While Blessed Petra of St. Joseph worked on her shrine dedicated to St. Joseph, Antoni Gaudi received theological guidance from a holy priest regarding the construction of the *Sagrada Familia* Basilica. That priest was St. José Manyanet (1833–1901). He was a zealous and devout priest who was very devoted to the Holy Family; he founded two religious communities dedicated to the Holy Family (Sons of the Holy Family and Missionary Daughters of the Holy Family). He also wrote many books about the Holy Family and was known for his zeal in preaching on this mystery of the faith. He was canonized in 2004 and is known as the "Apostle of the Holy Family."

Divine Providence was at work in all these things. These papal writings and the founding of new movements, associations, confraternities, and religious communities dedicated to St. Joseph and the Holy Family and the holy men and women who promoted new ways of being devoted to the Holy Family were all a sign that God was preparing the world for the many attacks against the family that would occur in the 20th and 21st centuries.

Now is the time to promote and defend the family and the Holy Family! Now is the time to be consecrated to the Holy Family! This is why we need another 33 Day consecration book. It's time for consecration to Jesus, Mary, and Joseph, the Holy Family. They're our way out of the mess we're in. They're the answer! They're the blueprint and model for happiness and holiness. With their guidance, and by consecrating ourselves to them, we can help restore order and common sense to a straying civilization.

33 Days to the Holy Family follows a pattern similar to all the other 33 Day consecration books. It's a book for everyone — individuals, families, parishes, prayer groups, etc. It's not an academic book but presents an easy formula for you to follow daily. Once you pick a start date, simply follow the instructions for each day until you reach Day 33 and consecrate yourself to the Holy Family. We have provided a consecration chart on page 16 that offers suggestions for when to start and finish so that your consecration day occurs on a liturgical feast associated with the Holy Family. It's that simple.

As you embark on this 33-day journey, ask the Holy Spirit to guide you and inspire you to always live under the watchful care of the Holy Family. Let the journey begin!

Consecration Chart

START OF THE 33 DAYS	FEAST DAY	CONSECRATION DAY
December 22	Feast of the Holy Spouses	January 23
January 1	Presentation of the Lord	February 2
February 15*	Solemnity of St. Joseph	March 19
February 21**	Annunciation	March 25
March 30	St. Joseph the Worker	May 1
April 11	Our Lady of Fatima	May 13
July 16	Our Lady of Knock	August 17
September 30	All Saints	November 1
November 6	Immaculate Conception	December 8
November 8	Our Lady of Loreto	December 10
November 23	Christmas	December 25
November***	Holy Family	December

* During a leap year, when February has 29 days, the starting date is February 16.

** During a leap year, when February has 29 days, the starting date is February 22.

*** The Solemnity of the Holy Family generally falls on the first Sunday after Christmas. If Christmas itself is on a Sunday, be sure to check what day the bishops designate as the Solemnity of the Holy Family and begin your consecration 32 days before the consecration date (Day 33).

THE CONSECRATION

DAY 1

Why a Consecration to the Holy Family?

> The human family on earth is an image of the divine family in heaven. This is what transmits God's plan from one generation to another. This is what spreads God's love and his word down through the generations. The collapse of the family means the ruin of the Lord's plan for humanity, that is to say, a breakdown that removes salvation and sanctity from human beings. Every family is a Holy Family because it is in the image of the Triune God. The deformation of the family means the deformation of God's image. The family carries the torch and the Book from generation to generation so that the world might continue to be illuminated by the light of the Lord. The family is the cord that ties human beings to one another through history, so that humanity might grow and multiply. If this cord is cut and humanity is separated from its history, the generations will be lost without history or identity. The family gives humanity its human identity and imprints the image of God on it. It safeguards human memory. Men without a family are men without a memory. Man deprived of memory goes around in circles. Humanity without memory stagnates in history and dies.[1]
>
> — St. Charbel Makhlouf

It doesn't get any clearer than that, does it? Sometimes it takes a saint to state the obvious. In essence, what St. Charbel is saying is that without the family mankind is in ruins. To prevent this from happening, we must return to the blueprint of the family, namely, the Holy Family. To do this, what better way than through a 33-day consecration to Jesus, Mary, and Joseph? This will help us to better understand, know, and love them. In turn, loving the Holy Family will help us to better understand and appreciate the importance of the family in society and secure the future of mankind.

The times are difficult, but we can do something about it. We can turn to Jesus, Mary, and Joseph and get back to the basics of how God intended us to live and grow in virtue. Now is the time for consecration to the Holy Family!

The Attack on the Family

It's simply undeniable that a demonic attack is being waged against the family today. Satan knows well that if the family falls, we all fall. The family unit is the basis of a peaceful and harmonious civilization, the bedrock of a just and loving society. Without the family, chaos erupts, charity is lost, and natural and supernatural virtues are unable to flourish and multiply. It's no wonder that the longest-lived Fatima visionary, Venerable Lucia dos Santos, once made the following powerful statement to a cardinal: "The final battle between the Lord and the kingdom of Satan will be about Marriage and the Family."[2] Take note: According to this saintly visionary of Fatima, the final battle between good and evil is not about ecology, climate change, immigration, or so-called cultural colonization. No. What destroys civilization and mankind's proper understanding of God and His ways is the colonization of evil in the minds and hearts of men, women, and children. This is why the destruction of the family is Satan's final and greatest attempt to distort and destroy God's image in us. If we fail to realize this and place the majority of our efforts to "fix" humanity in temporal affairs and mundane concerns, it's a sign that we're near the point of no return. And we aren't far from it. For example, worldwide birthrates are at an all-time low, the majority of Christians now practice some form of contraception, and Christian countries around the world have lost their identities and are rapidly fading away. Christendom is dead.

We find ourselves at a turning point in human history. Modern philosophers often refer to our times as the post-human era. Technology has replaced relationships, social media has decreased social virtue, and the very definition of marriage and family is left to the secular rulers of our day to determine. The battle over the family is raging. The spirit of darkness has pervaded practically every human institution, including universities, the entire medical field, all areas of science, politics, the military, and the majority of workplaces. Sadly, there are even many areas of the Church where various forms of darkness and anti-family ideology are being promoted and promulgated. The confusion and destruction are everywhere. We're in a huge mess.

Yes, it's *that* bad. Consider the words of a saintly Pope, John Paul II:

> Unfortunately various programs backed by very powerful resources nowadays seem to aim at the breakdown of the family. At times it appears that concerted efforts are being made to present as "normal" and attractive, and even to glamourize, situations which are in fact "irregular." Indeed, they contradict "the truth and love" which should inspire and guide relationships between men and women, thus causing tensions and divisions in families, with grave consequences particularly for children. The moral conscience becomes darkened; what is true, good, and beautiful is deformed; and freedom is replaced by what is actually enslavement.[3]

This holy Polish Pope who lived through, and fought against, communism, socialism, Marxism, fascism and a dozen other worldly ideologies knows what he's talking about. It's why he wrote his powerful *Letter to Families* in 1994. He knew the severity of the battle. Sadly, after his pontificate things have not gotten better but worse. Marriage has been re-defined in many countries; people in so-called homosexual marriages, which are unnatural and immoral in and of themselves, now have the right to adopt children; abortion rates have increased globally; new forms of contraception are flourishing; and those who defend and promote the truth of marriage and family life are unceasingly ridiculed, persecuted, and cancelled.

The Attack on the Holy Family

For the devil, the attack on the family is only the means to an end. The ultimate goal of the evil one is to attack and destroy the Holy Family. Remember this: The devil hates God more than anything else. In his twisted mind, destroying humanity isn't good enough for the devil. He wants to conquer and destroy God. He can't, of course, but the devil is a dreamer. Stuck in eternal fire, Lucifer never stops desiring the destruction of light and life and wants to make a mockery of all that is good, true, and beautiful. He can't get God Himself, and so he seeks to destroy God's plan for the human race by destroying the family, both human and divine. It's been this way since the beginning of time and continues happening with the New Covenant in Jesus Christ.

Pope St. Paul VI and Pope Leo XIII tell us the following about the Holy Family:

> We see that at the beginning of the New Testament, as at the beginning of the Old, there is a married couple. But whereas Adam and Eve were the source of evil which was unleashed on the world, Joseph and Mary are the summit from which holiness spreads all over the earth. The Savior began the work of salvation by this virginal and holy union.[4]

> When God in his mercy determined to accomplish the work of man's renewal, which some had so many long ages awaited, he appointed and ordained this work in such wise that its very beginning might

> shew to the world the august spectacle of a Family which was known to be divinely constituted; that therein all men might behold a perfect model, as well of domestic life as of every virtue and pattern of holiness: for such indeed was the Holy Family of Nazareth.[5]

Both mankind's fall from grace and God's plan for the sanctification and redemption of humanity in Christ start with a family. God ordained it this way. The Virgin Mary is essential to this plan. Saint Joseph is too. Along with all the saints and holy angels in Heaven they participate in the great battle of life. The devil knows that the family is at the center of God's plan for redemption too, and he also fights with all his minions to destroy the light. Do you know it? Do you understand the severity of this issue? Are you on the side of God or the side of the devil? Are you part of the solution, or are you part of the problem? In other words, by the way you live and conduct yourself in society, are you cooperating with God in the promulgation of the family, or are you fighting against God and His plan and knowingly or unknowingly making things worse by promoting falsehoods? Where is your allegiance? Are you for life, or are you for death?

These are tough questions, aren't they? But they need to be asked. And they need to be answered. The battle over the family is the "battle of battles," and it must be taken seriously. For this reason, now is the time for God's children to get their lives in order, seek understanding and knowledge, and get back to the foundations of the faith. Extolling the Holy Family and the importance of the family in civilization and society will help lead the nations back to reason and godliness. It's time to go on the offensive!

Consecration: The Spiritual Offensive

The great Marian saint and martyr of love St. Maximilian Kolbe often informed the members of his *Militia Immaculata* that they were to be on the offensive in their quest to lead souls to Jesus through Mary. Defense is good, but offense is better. You never gain ground playing defense. You move forward playing offense. Saint Maximilian encouraged those consecrated to Mary to be on the offense and hunt for souls, bringing everyone to Mary so that she can bring them to Jesus. Every saint knows that true devotion to Mary is the fastest, easiest, and surest way to know and love Jesus.

In the current climate of spiritual mediocrity and moral decay, we, too, need to be on the offensive. Fight fire with fire! If the family and the Holy Family are under attack, attack in return! What kind of an attack? Certainly not an attack with earthly weapons inflicting physical harm. Our battle is spiritual and we overcome evil with the spiritual weapons of prayer, truth, mercy, and sacrificial love. Promote family life. Promote Jesus, Mary, and Joseph. Such a battle plan requires action, perseverance, ingenuity, sacrifice, and suffering, but it's what needs to be done. Don't run from the battle. Charge into the fire!

Consecration to the Holy Family is the spiritual offense that is needed today. The devil is tricky, and the sons and daughters of light must strive to beat him at his own game. When he attacks, we go harder, stronger, longer. We can suffer for the cause; he can't. Saint Maximilian Kolbe gave his life for a fellow prisoner. What can we give to promote truth and light? Saint Maximilian brought people to Jesus through the Immaculata. What can we do to restore and promote true family life in the world? We can exult and promote Jesus, Mary, and Joseph, the Holy Family!

> The family is the basis in the Lord's plan, and all the forces of evil aim to demolish it, because they know that in destroying it they will shake the foundations of God's plan. The war of the Evil One against the Lord is a war waged against the family. This latter war is the essence of his

war against the Lord, because the family is the image of God. Since the beginning of the creation of this universe, the wicked one has persistently tried to destroy the family, which is the foundation of God's plan. The family is the place where a human being enters into communication with God and with his brethren. Without the family, this relationship would be destroyed and nothing could compensate for it, and if a man tries to repair the relationship by human means, it will become fragile and misguided, and along with that, all humanity will be subject to an evil that will tilt it toward inevitable death. Uphold your families and guard them against the grudges of the Evil One by the presence of God. Protect them and preserve them by prayer, by understanding and forgiveness, by sincerity and fidelity. Safeguard the warmth of the family because all the warmth of the world will not make up for it.[6]

— St. Charbel Makhlouf

Read the Introduction (page 11).

Pray the Veni Sancte Spiritus (page 219).

DAY 2
Litany of the Holy Family

> O God of infinite goodness and kindness, who has seen fit to call us to this family, give us the grace to venerate Jesus, Mary, and Joseph so that, imitating them in this life, we may enjoy with them the life to come. We ask this through Jesus Christ, our Lord. Amen.[1]
>
> — Concluding Prayer of the Litany of the Holy Family

Encouraging veneration and imitation of Jesus, Mary, and Joseph is the purpose of *33 Days to the Holy Family*. The models the world offers are all flawed. Jesus is God, Mary is an immaculate creature, and St. Joseph is as close to perfect as any man can get. Indeed, it's a tradition of the Church that St. Joseph, although not immaculately conceived, was, however, immaculately born. What does that mean? It means that although he wasn't conceived immaculate in his mother's womb like the Blessed Virgin Mary, he was purified in the womb and born into the world without sin. This privilege was granted to several Old Testament prophets, as well as St. John the Baptist; and, that being the case, it was undoubtedly granted to St. Joseph as well due to the lofty mission entrusted to him of being the earthly father of Jesus and the chaste spouse of the Virgin Mary.

In life, no matter what culture or milieu you live in, Jesus, Mary, and Joseph are, and will always remain, the model for family life and Christian living. If you make them the pattern for your family life and daily living, you will grow in holiness and virtue. You will help humanity to become better and godlier. As the saying goes, like is attracted to like. The apple doesn't fall far from the tree. And so it is with the Holy Family. For us, they are a mold. If you allow yourself to become docile to the movements of the Holy Spirit, you will find yourself conforming to the pattern of Jesus, Mary, and

Joseph. By venerating and imitating them in this life, you also may enjoy the beatific vision with them in Heaven.

The Importance of Prayer

To know, love, and imitate Jesus, Mary, and Joseph, you must talk to them and get to know them in a deeper way. For this reason, prayer is essential. Any type of consecration to the Holy Family that doesn't involve prayer might impart factual knowledge but will remain lifeless and sterile, unable to help you advance toward your goal — conformity to Jesus, Mary, and Joseph. For this reason, you need to make *33 Days to the Holy Family* a prayerful journey. Try to attend Mass more often than just on Sunday, go to Confession sometime during the 33 days, and think about their example and speak with them throughout your day. If you don't do this, don't expect to get much out of the consecration. What you put into it is what you will get out of it.

Many people start a consecration but never finish it. They get distracted and discouraged, miss a day (or two or three), and give up. Some leave it as the last thing they do in the day and eventually discontinue the journey out of tiredness. Don't be one of them. You can do this! Persevere! If you miss a day or two, make it up. It's not that hard. Don't leave it as the last thing you do in your day when you are already tired and just want to go to bed. Give the consecration priority in your life.

The devil doesn't want you to persevere. Shame the devil and see it through. Fight fire with fire! Prayer is fire. If you have a busy work schedule and family life and find it impossible to attend Mass on days other than Sunday, okay. But be faithful to the Sunday obligation. If you don't want to go to Confession to your local priest for some reason, okay. Drive to another parish in your area and go there. Take the consecration seriously, and you will reap the rewards of being renewed in mind, body, and soul, and in hope, charity, and joy!

If you want to lose weight or gain muscle, you know that you have to discipline yourself and observe a daily regimen. It's not easy; it's not meant to be. No pain, no gain. It's the same with spiritual growth. No prayer, no growth. This doesn't mean you have to become a monk or nun to consecrate yourself to the Holy Family. No. But what it does mean is that you need to observe a daily regimen of prayer. Take the time, make the time, and you will be blessed!

> There is nothing the devil fears so much, or so much tries to hinder, as prayer.[2]
>
> — St. Philip Neri

The Litany of the Holy Family

> Pronounce often and with great confidence the names of Jesus, Mary, and Joseph. Their names bring peace, love, health, blessings, majesty, glory, admiration, joy, happiness, and veneration. Their holy names are a blessing to angels and men, and a terror to demons. Christians should always have the names of Jesus, Mary, and Joseph in their hearts and on their lips.[3]
>
> — St. Bartolo Longo

Again, the saints know what they are talking about. At one time in his life, St. Bartolo Longo was an ordained priest of Satan and worshiped the devil. Yes, you read that right. But through repentance, prayer (especially the Rosary), and the power of Jesus, Mary, and Joseph, he was able to beat the devil and become a very holy man. And he was a layman, a lawyer by profession. If a man who once worshipped the devil can become holy, so can you.

Perhaps you're not good at prayer. Okay, fine. We're going to make it super easy for you, too easy almost. To ensure that you pray while making this consecration, you will be required to pray the Litany of the Holy Family at the end of each daily reading. This should take you no longer than three to five minutes. Easy.

Surprisingly, the Church doesn't yet have an official Litany of the Holy Family, so we have researched and adapted several versions used by sanctioned Catholic organizations for the purposes of this consecration. We pray that someday the Church will have an officially approved Litany of the Holy Family, but until then, the version you will pray daily as part of your consecration is a blending of the litanies found in the *Manual of the Archconfraternity of the Holy Family*[4] (canonically erected in the mid-19th century in Belgium with the help of the Redemptorist Fathers) and the one used by the Missionaries of the Holy Family (a religious community founded by the Servant of God Fr. John Berthier in 1895) in *Holy Family Prayer Book*.[5] We hope and pray you will be inspired by this litany. It's a beautiful prayer. It's such a lovely prayer that we decided to base the entire consecration around the titles provided in it. We start with the first title of the litany on Day 3 and present each subsequent title included in it on the days that follow, providentially ending on Day 33.

Knowing and Loving the Holy Family

> When Jesus, Mary, and Joseph are invoked in the home, charity is likely to be maintained in the family through their example and heavenly entreaty; a good influence is thus exerted over conduct; the practice of virtue is thus incited; and thus the hardships which are everywhere and want to harass mankind, are both mitigated and made easier to bear.[6]
>
> — Pope Leo XIII

You can't love what you don't know. You can't imitate what you don't know either. Therefore, if you want to love and imitate the Holy Family, you need to get to know them. That's what we hope *33 Days to the Holy Family* helps you to accomplish, namely, knowing Jesus, Mary, and Joseph so that you love and imitate them.

Some people might think that this consecration method is only for families who want to consecrate themselves to the Holy Family. It's not. While families are certainly encouraged to consecrate themselves to the Holy Family, this consecration is meant for everyone and is a means for individuals, engaged couples, families, widows, etc., to be consecrated to the Holy Family. Everyone, no matter their vocation, age, or state in life, needs them. No one should be excluded from consecrating themselves to the Holy Family, and we want to encourage everyone to do so.

Starting tomorrow (Day 3), the meat and potatoes of the consecration begin. The preliminaries are out of the way, and it's time to learn, grow, and love Jesus, Mary, and Joseph. Are you ready? The spiritual growth, peace, and hope you will be given are going to be off the charts. You can't go wrong with the Holy Family. Not only will you come to know and love them, you will also learn how to imitate and resemble them.

Let's go!

What we love we shall grow to resemble.[7]

— St. Bernard of Clairvaux

Pray the Litany of the Holy Family (page 207).

DAY 3

God, the Father of Heaven, have mercy on us

> To all of us, your children, grant, O merciful Father, that we may enter into a heavenly inheritance with the Blessed Virgin Mary, Mother of God, with Blessed Joseph, her Spouse, and with your Apostles and Saints in your kingdom. There, with the whole of creation, freed from the corruption of sin and death, may we glorify you through Christ our Lord, through whom you bestow on the world all that is good.
>
> — Eucharistic Prayer IV

God the Father loves you. He loves you so much that He sent His Son into the world to save you. But saving you is not all the Father sent His Son to do for you. He sent His Son to save you *and* make you a child of God.

"Child of God" is not just a nice phrase. It's meant literally. We're saved through adoption into the Holy Family and, through the Holy Family, the family of God the Father. Through Jesus, you are able to have a filial relationship with God the Father. Through Jesus, His Son, you can cry out, "Abba, Father!" Through Jesus, we become sons and daughters of God and members of His covenant family, able to legally inherit from our Heavenly Father. This is why the Eucharistic Prayer above describes our "heavenly inheritance." Eternal life in Heaven — this is our inheritance, the consequence of our adoption.

You were created to be a child of God; it's the very purpose for which you exist. And there is only one way to the Father: Jesus Christ (see Jn 14:6). Only Jesus has the power to take you to the Father. Yet, in God's merciful love, both the Virgin Mary and St. Joseph play a very important role in your spiritual growth and journey to the Father.

It's all about the Heavenly Father!

> For one and all are we destined by our birth and adoption to enjoy, when this frail and fleeting life is ended, a supreme and final good in heaven, and to the attainment of this every endeavor should be directed.[1]
>
> — Pope Leo XIII

Everything, *everything*, even down to your tiniest toe, should be ordered to God the Father. He is our "supreme and final good." He is the end of all our strivings, the ultimate goal of all our desires. The "First Principle and Foundation" of our entire creation and existence on earth, according to St. Ignatius of Loyola, is "to praise, reverence, and serve God, and by doing this, to save [our] souls."[2]

It's all about the Heavenly Father. Everything must be ordered to Him. This reordering begins with our adoption into God's family, the slow restoration of the human family to God's family. This is the purpose of the Incarnation of the God-Man. God created an earthly family for His Son, the Holy Family. God became part of this family so that we could become members of the Holy Family. The Holy Family, through adoption, became our bridge to the Heavenly Father.

Consecration to the Holy Family will bring you closer to God the Father

God, in His Divine Mercy, created the Holy Family to bring us closer to Himself. Jesus was "constituted the Head of the whole human family in the womb of the Blessed Virgin."[3] Therefore, through rebirth and Baptism in Christ, the whole human family is brought into the womb of the Blessed Virgin Mary. Through adoption, we become members of the Holy Family, brothers and sisters of Jesus, spiritual children of Mary and Joseph.

Think about that. God loves us so much, has so much mercy for us and desires closeness with us so much that He draws us out of the very wombs of our mothers toward His heavenly family. The infinite gravity of the God-Man, Jesus, pulls the entire human family to Himself, as the new epicenter of every genealogy and family tree that ever was. Consecration to the Holy Family brings us to God the Father!

To the Heavenly Father through the Holy Family

God the Father draws all men to Himself through Jesus, Mary, and Joseph. God desires to draw all families, all bloodlines, back to His own holy Bloodline. This began in the womb of Mary and was completed on the Cross. In Mary, the New Eve and mother of all the living, the divided human family is again united in one bloodline, the Sacred Blood of Jesus. Through His Blood, Jesus made the Jews and Gentiles one blood, one family, by "breaking down the wall of partition … in his flesh."[4]

Through Jesus' paschal sacrifice on the Cross, we are able to drink His Blood in the Eucharist. His Blood mingles with our blood. Our bloodline binds to His Bloodline. His Blood contains His life; and, if we are faithful to Him, trust in Him, and abide by His teachings, we will be resurrected with Him to eternal life with the Heavenly Father.

The Holy Family is essential to God's plan of salvation. Through our adoption in the covenant of the Holy Family, we are able to share in God's own life. We become blood relatives of God, heirs of eternal life and of the Kingdom of Heaven.

Pray the Litany of the Holy Family (page 207).

DAY 4

God the Son, Redeemer of the World, have mercy on us

> When God in his mercy decided to carry out the work of man's redemption, so long expected through the centuries, he arranged to perform his task in such a way that in its beginnings it might show forth to the world the august spectacle of a divinely founded family ... In this all men were to behold the perfect exemplar of domestic society as well as of all virtue and holiness ... Such indeed was the family of Nazareth. In its bosom was concealed the Sun of justice, awaiting in anticipation the time when his full splendors should shine in all the nations — Christ our God, our Savior, together with his Virgin Mother and Joseph ... A benign providence established the Holy Family in order that all Christians in whatever walk of life or situation might have a reason and an incentive to practice every virtue, provided they fix their gaze on the Holy Family.[1]
>
> — Pope Leo XIII

God the Son redeemed the world. This redemption began with a family and was accomplished through a family, the Holy Family. This is no small detail about Christianity and its existence. It didn't happen randomly but was the intentional, deliberate plan of Almighty God. In His infinite mercy, God arranged His entire plan of creation, redemption, and sanctification around the institution of the family in general and the Family of Nazareth in particular, with Jesus at the center of it all.

It's all about Jesus!

Everything depends on Jesus Christ. He's the center of the universe, the reason for our existence, and the hope of all men. Without Jesus, we're unable to enter Heaven. Without Jesus, we're unable to atone for our sins and receive the Holy Spirit. Hence, by God's eternal decree, the salvation of all men depends upon Jesus Christ.

How is this accomplished? Through the family, in particular the Holy Family. Pope St. Paul VI explained it this way:

> Nazareth is the school in which we begin to understand the life of Jesus. It is the school of the Gospel. Here we learn to observe, to listen, to meditate, and to penetrate the profound and mysterious meaning of that simple, humble, and lovely manifestation of the Son of God. And perhaps we learn almost imperceptibly to imitate him. Here we learn the method by which we can come to understand Christ. Here we discover the need to observe the milieu of His sojourn among us — places, period of time, customs, language, religious practices, all of which Jesus used to reveal Himself to the world.[2]

In 2004, Pope St. John Paul II remarked on the Feast of the Holy Family, "The Son of God prepared himself to carry out his redeeming mission [by] living a hard-working and hidden life in the holy house of Nazareth."[3] Jesus chose to incorporate the Holy House of Nazareth into His plan for the redemption and salvation of mankind. He could have saved us in a different way, but He didn't. He chose the family; He loves the family! The course of salvation passes through the family; and, as a result, Jesus unites "his Incarnation with every man and woman … to sanctify human families."[4] Jesus wants to be in every family, and He wants everyone to be in His family.

The Redeemer came to us through a family

> The Redeemer of the world chose the family as the place for his birth and growth, thereby sanctifying this fundamental institution of every society.[5]
>
> — Pope St. John Paul II

Jesus' work of redemption began in the Holy Family, and it continues in every human family. Yes, Jesus is free to redeem people how He wishes, but His established and normative way is through the family. We learn this lesson in the biblical episode when the boy Jesus is found in the Temple. "After three days [Mary and Joseph] found him in the temple, sitting among the teachers, listening to them and asking them questions; and all who heard him were amazed at his understanding and his answers" (Lk 2:46–47).

Jesus could have chosen to stay among the teachers in the Temple and initiate His public ministry there. He could have left home at that point and saved the world — but He didn't. Instead, Jesus *purposefully* returns to His family in Nazareth, and there "increased in wisdom and in stature, and in favor with God and man" (Lk 2:52) under the watchful care of His parents. Jesus chose this path specifically and strategically.

To Jesus through the Holy Family

Why the family? Much less, *this* family, a poor family in Nazareth, which was considered a backwater town in Israel? The reason is because this location fulfills an important messianic prophecy. Do you remember when Nathanael mocks Jesus' birthplace, saying, "Can anything good come out of Nazareth?" (Jn 1:46)? This short remark is actually the fulfillment of one of the most important messianic prophecies of the Old Testament, which was repeated and echoed by every major prophet from Isaiah to Daniel. This is the prophecy that the Messiah will be a "righteous branch." Here is Isaiah's statement of it:

> There shall come forth a shoot from the stump of Jesse,
> and a branch shall grow out of his roots.
> And the Spirit of the LORD shall rest upon him,
> the spirit of wisdom and understanding,
> the spirit of counsel and might,
> the spirit of knowledge and the fear of the LORD.
> And his delight shall be in the fear of the LORD.
> (Is 11:1–3)

What is the "stump of Jesse"? Jesse was King David's father. The tree that grew from Jesse was David, his children, and the kings who succeeded him. This was David's family tree. When the line of kings was broken, the tree was cut down, leaving only a stump. The "shoot" springing forth from the "stump of Jesse" is the New David, the Messiah, his royal descendant who will restore Israel. The Messiah will restore David's kingly bloodline, the royal family tree. The family will be reborn, and new life will spring from the Holy Family.

How do Nazareth and the Holy Family fit into this new "family tree" which will grow from the "stump of Jesse"? Well, Nazareth has two very important meanings.

The first one is "branch." Jesus, the "righteous branch," was raised in the city of the "branch." The second meaning is equally revealing. "Nazareth" also means "to consecrate." We observe this in the "Nazarite" vow taken by St. John the Baptist, who was specially consecrated to the Lord. The Gospel of Matthew confirms this prophecy: "And [Joseph] went and dwelt in a city called Nazareth, that what was spoken by the prophets might be fulfilled, 'He [the Messiah] shall be called a *Nazarene*'" (Mt 2:23, emphasis added). This is how we are bound to Jesus through the Holy Family. "Consecration" grafts us onto the Holy Family Tree of Jesse and King David, and Jesus, Mary, and Joseph of Nazareth. This is why Jesus chose the Family of Nazareth. This is how the Holy Family fits into God's plan for the redemption of all mankind. This is what makes us part of Christ's own family.

Pray the Litany of the Holy Family (page 207).

DAY 5

God, the Holy Spirit, have mercy on us

> The origin which [Christ] took in the womb of the Virgin He has given to the baptismal font: He has given to water what He had given to His mother — the power of the Most High — and the overshadowing of the Holy Spirit (see also Lk. 1:35), which was responsible for Mary's bringing forth the Savior, has the same effect, so that water may regenerate the believer.[1]
>
> — St. Leo the Great

Overshadowed by the Holy Spirit, Mary carried Jesus' Body in her womb. Jesus' Mystical Body is all of us, the baptized. Therefore, the waters of Mary's womb are, in a mystical sense, the first waters of Baptism. In his encyclical *Marialis Cultus*, Pope St. Paul VI writes, "[The Church] reflects on the singular dignity of the Virgin who, through the action of the Holy Spirit, has become Mother of the Incarnate Word, … [and the Church expresses her devotion] in burning love … when she considers the spiritual motherhood of Mary towards all members of the Mystical Body."[2] This is how the Holy Spirit draws us into the Holy Family through the waters of Baptism. In Baptism, we are reborn as children of Mary and Joseph. In a very real sense, therefore, we become members of the Holy Family through the Holy Spirit.

It's all about the Holy Spirit!

The Holy Spirit wants you to know and love the Holy Family of Jesus, Mary, and Joseph. Never was the Holy Spirit more active in a family than He was in the Holy Family. Jesus was conceived by the Holy Spirit, who "overshadowed" the Blessed Mother at the Annunciation (Lk 1:35), and St. Joseph was given charge over them both, to protect and guard them from Satan. Saint Bartolo Longo was so bold as to refer to St. Joseph as the "Vicar of the Holy Spirit":

> Saint Joseph, Vicar of the Holy Spirit in fulfilling the duties of your wonderful marriage with Mary, introduce the Holy Spirit to my will in order to ignite it with God's holy love. Present my will to the Most Holy Trinity so that my desires may always be at God's disposal. Offer my heart to God so that he may dwell in it as on a throne of love and mercy. Present the movements of my soul and all the affections of my heart to God so that through your intercession I will always be faithful to the grace and inspirations of the Holy Spirit. Amen.[3]

Jesus' mother and earthly father never did anything without seeking the direction of the Holy Spirit. The Virgin Mary was espoused to the Holy Spirit. Through their union, Jesus came into the world. Saint Joseph's docility to the Holy Spirit made it possible for him to communicate with God even when he slept, through his dreams. The Holy Spirit was active and deeply involved in the life of each person of the Holy Family, whether divine or human. It should be the same with us.

The Holy Spirit is the Sanctifier

> [T]he sanctifying intervention of the Spirit in the Virgin of Nazareth was a culminating moment of the Spirit's action in the history of salvation. ... [The Church Fathers] saw in the Spirit's intervention an action that consecrated and made fruitful Mary's virginity and transformed her into the "Abode of the King" or "Bridal Chamber of the Word," the "Temple" or "Tabernacle of the Lord," the "Ark of the Covenant" or "the Ark of Holiness," titles rich in biblical echoes.[4]

— Pope St. Paul VI

It's important to understand the many ways that the Holy Spirit intervened in history to sanctify the people of God. So many of these instances point to the Holy Family, long before the events of the Gospels took place. We can't understand many of the descriptions of Jesus, Mary, and Joseph and the events that occurred in their lives without understanding their connections to the Old Testament. These connections will be further explained in subsequent days of this consecration.

One of the primary examples of the Holy Spirit's sanctifying work in the Old Testament was the Holy Spirit "overshadowing" Moses' Ark of the Covenant. It's no mistake that the same word is only used to describe the Glory Cloud "overshadowing" the Ark of the Covenant (Ex 25:20) and the Holy Spirit "overshadowing" the Virgin Mary at the Annunciation (Lk 1:35). Clearly the Virgin Mary is the New Ark of the Covenant.

The Holy Spirit sanctified, protected, and guided the people of Israel through the presence of the Glory Cloud and the Ark of the Covenant. The Ark of the Covenant contained the instruments of Israel's sanctification. The Glory Cloud barred the advance of Pharaoh's chariots and served as a warning of God's power to the nations and as a beacon throughout all the time Israel wandered in the wilderness. In the coming days, we will see how the Holy Spirit fulfills all these actions through the New Ark of the Covenant, Mary, and her guardian and custodian, St. Joseph.

To the Holy Spirit through the Holy Family

I beg you, holy Virgin, that I may have Jesus from the Holy Spirit, by whom you brought Jesus forth. May my soul receive Jesus through the Holy Spirit by whom your flesh conceived Jesus. May I love Jesus in the Holy Spirit in whom you adore Jesus as Lord and gaze upon him as your Son.[5]

— St. Ildephonsus of Toledo

> In the Blessed Virgin Mary there takes place the miracle of God's union with creation. From the moment such a union took place, the Holy Spirit grants no graces, the Father, through the Son and Spirit, infuses no supernatural life into the soul except through the Mediatrix of all graces, the Immaculata, with her consent [and]... cooperation.[6]
>
> — St. Maximilian Kolbe

This is a very strong statement from St. Maximilian Kolbe: "the Holy Spirit grants no graces" without Mary's cooperation. At her Immaculate Conception, "the Holy Spirit established his dwelling in her soul, took possession of it absolutely."[7] The Holy Spirit dwells in the Blessed Virgin far more perfectly than He did even in the Ark of the Covenant. Also, because of their sacramental marriage, St. Joseph shares in all the graces of his immaculate spouse. And, of course, the Holy Spirit dwells perfectly within Jesus, the Son of God.

This is why we go to the Holy Spirit through the Holy Family. Jesus and the Holy Spirit came into the world through the Holy Family. They are our bridge, our conduit, our aqueduct to the Holy Spirit as well.

It's also no coincidence that the Blessed Mother was present when the Holy Spirit descended on the apostles and disciples at Pentecost (Acts 1:14). When we consecrate ourselves to the Holy Family, we are uniting ourselves to the epicenter of all graces, the locus of all the Holy Spirit's work for the whole world and for all time. Just as St. Joseph shared in all the Blessed Virgin Mary's graces through the covenant of marriage, we share in all these graces through the family covenant.

By consecrating ourselves to the Holy Family, we are making our home in the abiding place of all graces, the tabernacle of the Holy Spirit. Jesus says, "Abide in me, and I in you. As the branch cannot bear fruit by itself, unless it abides in the vine, neither can you, unless you abide in me" (Jn 15:4). Jesus is the "righteous branch," the source of the new family tree established at Nazareth — which, as we discussed yesterday, means both "branch" and "consecration." Abide with the Holy Family at Nazareth.

Pray the Litany of the Holy Family (page 207).

DAY 6

Holy Trinity, One God, have mercy on us

> Our God in his deepest mystery is not a solitude, but a family.[1]
>
> — Pope St. John Paul II

> The human family, in a certain sense, is an icon of the Trinity because of its interpersonal love and the fruitfulness of this love.[2]
>
> — Pope Benedict XVI

The Holy Trinity is a family, a holy family. They want you to be a member of their family. To make this happen, They have established a replica of the Trinity here on earth — an earthly trinity. The Holy Family is the earthly icon of the Holy Trinity. The earthly trinity consists of Jesus, Mary, and Joseph. Like the Holy Trinity, each person in the Holy Family is distinct yet united. The Holy Family's union is a covenant, a binding love that isn't self-seeking, but all-encompassing, a love which reaches out to each other and the entire world.

The Holy Family makes the invisible Trinity visible in the world. They make divine love understandable, even palpable. In a sense, they are the first Christian church. Membership in this family will prepare you for membership in God's eternal family in Heaven.

It's all about the Holy Trinity!

> Eternal God, eternal Trinity … you are a mystery as deep as the sea; the more I search, the more I find, and the more I find the more I search for you.[3]
>
> — St. Catherine of Siena

God is the most perfect family. This, of course, does not explain the mystery of the Trinity, but only deepens it. And the wonderful thing is, as St. Catherine of Siena explains above, that the more we search out the depths of the Holy Trinity, the more we find. We also find out more about love, the family, and the Holy Family.

First and foremost, God is the eternal Father in this most perfect family. He is *eternally* fathering. God the Father did not create the world, set all things in motion, and then leave, like a divine clockmaker. He is still creating, preserving us in existence every moment. He is eternally present.

The Creed describes God the Son as "begotten, not made, consubstantial with the Father." God the Son was never "created." There was never a time when He did not exist. He is *eternally* begotten of the Father. He is begotten from the Father as "light from light," the same substance ("consubstantial") as God the Father. If God the Father is eternally fathering, God the Son is eternally "son-ing," or in other words, being eternally begotten as the Son. Saint Anselm attempted to explain the Trinity as God the Father seeing Himself in a mirror, a living mirror, an eternal thought of His perfect understanding of Himself, His perfect self-*conception*.[4] God the Son is eternally reflecting the Father as the most perfect expression of His existence. This is the opposite of the Greek myth of Narcissus who lost himself by forever staring into his own reflection. Narcissus loved only himself. The Holy Trinity loves the other so perfectly that all creation is the fruit of this love.

The Father and the Son are an eternal gaze of love. This love is alive. It's a Divine Person, the Holy Spirit. Love is not merely perfect between the three Divine Persons; it is an entire Person, separate from the other two, but eternally proceeding from both Father and Son. Contained in this mystery is the perfect love of the family, the love to which every family, by its own procession from the Holy Trinity, aspires. The Holy Family is the human family that perfectly aspires to this love and attains it. By consecrating ourselves to the Holy Family, we join in their perfect ascent to the Holy Trinity.

The Holy Trinity is your Home

> For the Son of God became man so that we might become God.[5]
>
> — St. Athanasius

Our ultimate destination in life has always been the Holy Trinity. The Holy Trinity is our home. Adam was expelled from mankind's first home, the Garden of Eden, "lest he put forth his hand and take also of the Tree of Life, and eat, and live for ever" (Gen 3:22). Eating from the Tree of Life would have ultimately resulted in the divinization of Adam and Eve's family. Because of their sin, the original Holy Family was evicted from their home.

But God provided us with a New Tree of Life, a new *family* tree. The fruit of this New Tree of Life is the Eucharist — Jesus' Body, Blood, Soul, and Divinity and "the fruit of [Mary's] womb." By consuming Jesus in the Eucharist, we are divinized. We don't become gods of course. We're not polytheists. Rather, we become "partakers of the divine nature."[6] We can once again eat freely from the Tree of Life and return home to the Holy Trinity.

Saint Maximilian Kolbe explains:

> From the first moment of [the Blessed Virgin Mary's] existence, the Giver of graces, the Holy Spirit, established his dwelling in [her] soul, took possession of it absolutely, and permeated her so completely that the name of Bride of the Holy Spirit conveys but a pale, distant, imperfect, albeit truthful shadow of such union.[7]

We imitate Our Lady by giving ourselves entirely — our memory, understanding, will, and thoughts — to the Holy Trinity. One of the prayers of St. Francis de Sales illustrates this:

> I vow and consecrate to God all that is in me:
> My memory and my actions to God the Father;
> My understanding and my words to God the Son;
> My will and my thoughts to God the Holy Spirit.[8]

> When we give ourselves entirely to the Trinity, the Holy Trinity takes possession of us and establishes Their home in us. But we can't encompass the Holy Trinity. When the Persons of the Trinity make Their home in us, we return home.

To the Holy Trinity through the Holy Family

The Holy House of Nazareth is the New Eden, and it contains the New Tree of Life, the new family tree of the Holy Family.

Saint Joseph, your spiritual father, will help you become a true child of the Heavenly Father. The Virgin Mary, your spiritual mother, will help you become a true icon of the Holy Spirit, fully endowed with the fruits of your Baptism and Confirmation. Your spiritual parents will teach you how to love, pray, sacrifice, and work. They will teach you how to do the will of God. The pathway to Heaven is paved with virtues and adorned with the gifts of the Holy Spirit. Saint Joseph will "increase" the virtues in you. Mary will "magnify" the gifts of the Holy Spirit in you.

Membership in the Family of Nazareth — accepting St. Joseph as your father, Mary as your mother, and Jesus as your brother — is the surest, easiest, and quickest way for us to become "partakers of the divine nature."[9] Through the Holy Family, the Son of God, "wanting to make us sharers in his divinity, assumed our nature, so that he, made man, might make men gods."[10] This doesn't mean we become the fourth and fifth persons of the Trinity. It means we become fully immersed in the infinite depths of the Holy Trinity, which is love, truth, and beauty itself.

Pray the Litany of the Holy Family (page 207).

DAY 7

Jesus, Mary, and Joseph, have pity on us

> And he went down with them and came to Nazareth, and was obedient to them; and his mother kept all these things in her heart. And Jesus increased in wisdom and in stature, and in favor with God and man.
>
> — Lk 2:51–52

You belong to Jesus. He wants you to grow in virtue and holiness, that is, in true love of God and neighbor. To make this happen, you must imitate Jesus. In particular, the best way to do so is to imitate His total entrustment to Mary and Joseph.

When Mary and Joseph lost Jesus and found Him in the temple, He was a young boy. He could have remained where they found Him, "sitting among the teachers, listening to them and asking them questions" (Lk 2:46). Jesus could have remained in the Temple, His "Father's house," as He described it: "How is it that you sought me? Did you not know that I must be in my Father's house?" (Lk 2:49). Instead, Jesus chose to remain with the Holy Family. He entrusted Himself to them and consecrated Himself through them, "increasing in wisdom and in stature, and in favor with God and man" (Lk 2:52).

The Preeminence of Jesus, Mary, and Joseph

Jesus chose the humble Family of Nazareth over the Temple, which was the preeminent religious and governmental structure in the entire world for the Jews. This was the rebuilt Temple of Solomon, and it had embodied the hopes and dreams of every Jew for hundreds of years. For Jesus, however, "something greater than Solomon" was in Nazareth (Mt 12:42).

The heart of the Temple of Solomon was the Ark of the Covenant. The Prophet Jeremiah hid the Ark just before the Babylonian invasion (see 2 Macc 2:4–8). By the time Jesus was born, the Ark of the Covenant had been missing for hundreds of years. But Jesus knew where to find the New Ark of the Covenant: in Nazareth. It was the Virgin Mary and her Immaculate Heart.

Israel's glory under King David and King Solomon lasted only 80 years. Afterwards, it plunged into idolatry and sin. When Israel refused to return to God's covenant, the nation lost its preeminence, its land, and its kingdom. In 586 B.C., Nebuchadnezzar wiped out the last vestige of the glory of David and Solomon's reigns and carried Judah, the Southern Kingdom of Israel, into captivity in Babylon. But the line of kings was not broken, only lost. Jesus knew where to find the heir to the Kingdom of Israel. He found it in the royal fatherhood and Most Chaste Heart of St. Joseph.

Consecration to Jesus, Mary, and Joseph

Jesus, more than anyone else, wants to make the three Hearts of Nazareth — His Sacred Heart, the Immaculate Heart of Mary, and the Most Chaste Heart of St. Joseph — the center of your life. Jesus, more than anyone else, wants you to follow in His footsteps and imitate His love for Mary and Joseph. He wants you to love them as He did and as they loved each other.

The Virgin Mary and St. Joseph's love for Jesus is immeasurable, but so is their love for each other. They were spouses in every sense of the word, though virgins. Their love for each other was increased by their love of Jesus and proximity to Him, not decreased.

The Virgin Mary is St. Joseph's wife, queen, and the delight of his Heart. She is the only woman who could ever satisfy his Chaste Heart. As Adam was not fulfilled until he rested in a creature similar to himself (Eve), so, too, Joseph, the descendant of Adam, only rested when he found Mary, the New Eve.

When Joseph took Mary's hand in marriage, he consecrated himself to her and made a promise to treasure her femininity, especially her blessed virginity. He was her beloved provider, protector, and servant. He earnestly desires for her to be honored and loved by everyone. Likewise, when Mary took Joseph's hand in marriage, she consecrated herself to him and made a promise to treasure his masculinity, especially his blessed virginity. She was his beloved homemaker, nurturer, and servant. Mary made the house in Nazareth a home, and St. Joseph protected it. Mary earnestly desires for St. Joseph to be honored and loved by everyone.

Consecration to the Holy Family: The Divine Reset

Despite the promises of God and the faith of the Jews, the glory of Israel seemed dead and gone in the days of Jesus' birth. King Herod the Great had rebuilt the temple, but he was a false king, a puppet controlled by a far greater power, the Roman Empire. The glory and might of Rome had resulted in the *Pax Romana*, the longest period of peace in world history because Rome had utterly destroyed all its enemies.

However, a quiet rumbling that began in Nazareth totally upended and reset the powers and principalities of the whole world. The earthquake that began in Nazareth ultimately usurped Rome and the Prince of the World, Satan. Satan was caught by surprise because Jesus had been concealed in the Holy Family. When the dust settled, however, the New Temple of Jesus' Body alone remained standing, with the New Ark at its heart and the royal line of David, through Joseph, re-established in Christ the King.

The powers of darkness continue to attack the Church and each one of us, but the Holy Family remains. Even now, the Holy Family stands ready to intervene in your life with another divine reset.

Call on them, consecrate yourself to them, and that quiet rumbling will prevail against the evil in your life, too. The Holy Family will uproot the evil in your life and conceal you from Satan, beneath the cloak of St. Joseph and the mantle of the Virgin Mary.

Pray the Litany of the Holy Family (page 207).

DAY 8

Jesus, Mary, and Joseph, most worthy of our veneration, have pity on us

> Just as Mary, mother of the Savior, is spiritual mother to all Christians, Joseph looks on all Christians as having been confided to himself. He is the defender of the Holy Church, which is truly the House of God and the Kingdom of God on earth.[1]
>
> — Pope Leo XIII

> I know not how anyone can ponder on the sufferings, trials, and tribulations the Queen of Angels endured while caring for the Infant Jesus, without at the same time thanking St. Joseph for the services he rendered the Divine Child and his Blessed Mother.[2]
>
> — St. Teresa of Ávila

The Fourth Commandment instructs us, "Honor your father and your mother that your days may be long in the land which the Lord your God gives you" (Ex 20:12). What does it mean to "honor" our parents? The same word in the Old Testament is not just used for honoring your parents, but for *glorifying* the Lord God as well (Ps 50:15; 50:23). Clearly we owe high honor to our parents and our *adopted* parents, Mary and Joseph.

We are adopted into Jesus' own family through Baptism. We are brothers and sisters of Jesus and sons and daughters of Mary and Joseph. Venerating them, as we honor our parents, is not at all disrespectful of Jesus or distracting from the worship we owe Him. What brother would be offended if his younger siblings acted with reverence and obedience toward their mother and father? What man would be upset if another person wrote a hymn about his mother or placed roses at her feet? Likewise, what son would be disturbed if someone praised the virtues of his father? A person who honored a father or mother thus would not receive condemnation from the son. On the contrary, such a person would receive praise and tremendous favors. This is exactly what Jesus stands ready to do for those who honor Mary and St. Joseph and His Holy Family. Jesus will give them everything. Jesus stands ready to give you everything!

Latria, Hyperdulia, Protodulia

In Greek, there are specific terms to identify the different kinds of honor we owe to God, the saints, and the Blessed Mother and St. Joseph. First off is *latria* — this is worship due to God alone. Worship is a kind of honor distinct from veneration. There are several kinds of veneration: *dulia*, *hyperdulia*, and *protodulia*. *Dulia* is the veneration given to the holy angels and the saints. We venerate these figures as our role models and intercessors. We acknowledge and imitate their heroic lives of virtue and ask for their prayers.

Hyperdulia is a higher form of *dulia* that is reserved solely for the Virgin Mary. In *hyperdulia*, Mary is given an exceptional place of honor among all the saints and angels as the Mother of God (*Theotokos*). She is honored as the Queen of Saints and Queen of Angels. This honor is due to her critical role in salvation history, as she bore the Son of God.

Protodulia is a specific kind of *dulia* reserved for the veneration given to St. Joseph. The word "proto" means "first," as St. Joseph is considered to be first among the saints who are honored with the veneration of *dulia*.

Living a Pious Life Every Day

> Charity is so beautiful that it makes all our works pleasing to God, even the smallest and least valuable. If it is a sure sign that we love and honor God in the person of our neighbor, how much should we thank God for the grace and favor of having

> called us to an institution [the family] where we have so many means of exercising this divine virtue by the daily practice of the spiritual and corporal works of mercy? Therefore, we should fulfill with unalterable joy the functions that are designated to us, however painful and humble they may be and without any reservations and without any person excepted. Charity has the heart of a father for all, has compassion for all, and treats all with affection and benevolence.[3]
>
> — St. José Manyanet

Through the Holy Family, everyday life and all its little piddly tasks are transformed into stepping-stones to the heights of Heaven. We meditate on the Holy House of Nazareth to discover how to achieve great intimacy with Jesus in ordinary, everyday life. Jesus, Mary, and Joseph performed the same workaday tasks you do. They ate, drank, and slept. They cleaned the house, earned a living, prayed, and interacted with neighbors, just as you do. Jesus refers to all these daily chores in His parables because He lived them.

Jesus welcomes the righteous to His Kingdom, saying, "Come, O blessed of my Father, inherit the kingdom prepared for you from the foundation of the world; for I was hungry and you gave me food, I was thirsty and you gave me drink, I was a stranger and you welcomed me, I was naked and you clothed me, I was sick and you visited me, I was in prison and you came to me" (Mt 25:34–36). Jesus is listing the Corporal Works of Mercy that St. José Manyanet also mentions above. Jesus tells us, "Truly, I say to you, as you did it to one of the least of these my brethren, you did it to me" (Mt 25:40). Jesus tells us we are directly serving Him when we serve the least of His brethren. We may pay lip service to Jesus' words, but the Holy Family gives us a much deeper, more intimate, understanding of them when we consider that we are literally Jesus' brethren through adoption into the Holy Family.

When we think about the Corporal and Spiritual Works of Mercy,[4] we might think of doing them through secular institutions or church charities and confraternities like the Knights of Columbus or the Society of St. Vincent de Paul. But have you ever considered how the Blessed Mother and St. Joseph performed these works of mercy? We see Jesus through the poor, but Mary and Joseph beheld Jesus *face-to-face*, every day. Think of the Blessed Mother and St. Joseph with the Infant Jesus. When did Mary and Joseph see Jesus hungry, thirsty, and naked? Every time the Blessed Mother nursed Jesus and St. Joseph changed His swaddling clothes, they were performing works of mercy directly for Jesus Himself. Jesus was a stranger to this world, hated by King Herod and its rulers, and Mary welcomed Him into her own womb. The depths of intimacy we learn in the humble house of Nazareth are unfathomable. When we learn such intimacy with Jesus in the arms of the Holy Family, we discover why Jesus calls us to these Works of Mercy today. We begin to truly *see* Jesus in others, and others begin to recognize Jesus in us. Jesus becomes *familiar* to us and others through the Holy Family.

One practical way to rededicate our daily work and ordinary life as Works of Mercy, intimately united with the Holy Family, is to dedicate certain days of the week to the Holy Family. To help us do so, the Church has ancient traditions regarding the practice of setting aside certain days of the week to honor Jesus, Mary, and Joseph.

Sunday, Saturday, and Wednesday

Sunday is dedicated to Jesus, because it is the day of His Resurrection. Also, by ancient custom, we dedicate Saturday to the honor of the Virgin Mary and Wednesday in honor of St. Joseph. Saint Thomas Aquinas explains this, saying: "Since the Resurrection took place on a Sunday, we keep holy this day instead of the Sabbath as did the Jews of old. However, we also sanctify Saturday in honor of the glorious Virgin

Mary who remained unshaken in faith all day Saturday after the death of her Divine Son."[5]

Since Sunday is devoted to Jesus, it's also fitting to dedicate the day prior to His mother. Saint Alphonsus Liguori expounds on this idea, saying, "It is well known that Saturday has been set aside by the Church as Mary's Day because it was on the Sabbath after the death of her Son that she remained unshaken in her faith."[6] Saint Alphonsus describes how he, along with many other saints and holy people in the history of the Church, fasted on Saturdays in honor of the Blessed Mother. In return for his love and honor, the Blessed Mother bestowed on St. Alphonsus a great gift by preserving him from mortal sin until his death in 1787 at the age of 91.[7]

Pope St. John XXIII observed the custom of honoring St. Joseph on Wednesdays: "On Wednesdays do something also for St. Joseph, such as saying the usual prayers, reading some book about him, making some special mortification, in short offering everything to him."[8]

The custom of dedicating Wednesdays for devotion to St. Joseph has been popular at least since the end of the 17th century.[9] Wednesday represents the middle of the week, so it makes sense to put St. Joseph here, since he is an essential member of the Holy Family and worthy of a special day of the week dedicated to him. Blessed Concepción Cabrera de Armida encourages us, "Offer every Wednesday of the year to St. Joseph."[10]

Live and breathe with the Holy Family. Make these daily offerings a part of your life, and make your life an offering to the Holy Family. They will invite you into their home, the Holy House of Nazareth. We consecrate ourselves to the Holy Family in order to spend every day of the week, all of our ordinary daily lives, in their presence.

Pray the Litany of the Holy Family *(page 207).*

DAY 9

Jesus, Mary, and Joseph, called "The Holy Family" from all time, have pity on us

I will put enmity between you and the woman,
    and between your seed and her seed;
he shall bruise your head,
    and you shall bruise his heel.

— Gen 3:15

How can the Holy Family be called the Holy Family "from all time"? In the verse above, God announces to the original Holy Family, Adam and Eve — and to Satan, the serpent, as well — His entire plan for the redemption of mankind, that is, the whole Gospel. That is why this verse is called the *Protoevangelium* or "First Gospel." It announces the Gospel and the establishment of a new Holy Family at the beginning of time. It contains three prophecies, the *first* prophecies in all human history.

The first prophecy is "I will put enmity between you and the woman." "Enmity" means enemies. In the future there will be a woman who will be an enemy of Satan from her very beginning, that is, from her conception. She will be the Immaculate Conception. The very first prophecy in all human history is a prophecy of the Immaculate Conception. Let that sink in. This is why Jesus addresses Mary as "woman" (Jn 2:4) at the Wedding at Cana and from the Cross when He says, "Woman, behold your son" (Jn 19:26).

In the second prophecy, Jesus is described as "her seed," the seed of Mary. Everywhere else in the Bible, when somebody is described as a "seed" of his parents, it's as his father's seed.[1] Why is Jesus described as "her seed," without reference to a biological father? Because, of course, Jesus had no biological father. He was born of a virgin. This is the first prophecy of the Virgin Birth of Jesus. The third prophecy concerns Jesus and Mary together crushing Satan's skull.

Let's put all this together. From "all time," the Immaculate Conception was prophesied to be the Mother of the Messiah. The coming of the Holy Family was announced to our first parents right after they failed to be the Holy Family, thus losing their original holiness. As soon as the first family fell, God began to call into existence the Holy Family of Jesus, Mary, and Joseph, a future family which would not fall, but be holy — for all time.

Bethlehem: School of Faith, Hope, and Love

> The merciful God, in carrying out the work of the long-desired human redemption, wished to accomplish it in such a way that its beginning would be to show to the world a singular family, divinely constituted, in which all men could contemplate the most complete model of domestic society, of all virtue and holiness.[2]
>
> — Pope Leo XIII

The school of Bethlehem begins on the road. The enrollment announced by Caesar Augustus forces the Holy Family to travel to Bethlehem (Lk 2:1–5), despite Mary's pregnancy. The Holy Family undertakes this difficult, uncomfortable journey during the second or third trimester of her pregnancy. The virtues are on full display during this journey, particularly the theological virtues of faith, hope, and love.

Faith is "the assurance of things hoped for, the conviction of things not seen" (Heb 11:1). The ultimate unseen, invisible reality is God, and yet, with unshakable faith, the Holy Family is about to see God face-to-face in the Babe lying in the manger. Saint Paul also tells us about hope: "May the God of hope fill you with all joy and peace in believing, so that by the power of the Holy Spirit you may abound in hope" (Rom 15:13). Hope is the joy and peace experienced in the expectancy of God fulfilling his promises. Here are two *expectant* parents of the incarnation of God's promises, the Word of God itself. And so we pray, "Hail, Holy Queen, Mother of Mercy, our life, our sweetness, and our *hope*." Mary and Joseph are the parents of hope, and the Baby is its incarnation. "After this our exile," the prayer continues, Mary will "show unto us the blessed fruit of [her] womb, Jesus." We pray this because the Holy Family also suffered exile from their home in Nazareth. At the end of their road to Bethlehem, they, likewise, were shown the "blessed fruit" of Mary's womb. They beheld the face of Jesus.

Think now of the love — the glowing, radiant love — painted into all of man's depictions of the birth of Jesus. For ages, artists have exhausted their skills trying to depict the love born to the Holy Family at Bethlehem. Now the Holy Family invites us to dwell with them in this endless moment of tender love for the newborn Jesus, the revelation of all their faith and the fulfillment of all their hope, a moment prophesied for all time.

Egypt: School of Trust

Imagine yourself as St. Joseph. He's warned in a dream to flee from Bethlehem to Egypt (Mt 2:13–15). Saint Joseph trusts God without hesitation. Shortly thereafter, King Herod orders all the boys in Bethlehem 2 years old or younger to be killed (Mt 2:16–18). This was already a tumultuous time for St. Joseph, having traveled with his family from Nazareth to Bethlehem for the census. Now, they have to flee for their lives, not simply to a new city, but an entirely new country. Saint Joseph's forced move echoes that of his namesake, Joseph of Egypt, who was sold into slavery in Egypt. This is truly a time of trust for the Holy Family.

Imagine yourself to be Jesus' age. You've barely learned to walk, but now you're walking or being carried all the way to Egypt, crossing the same desert and wilderness in the Sinai peninsula where your ancestors wandered for so long. This is an exhausting time, but you trust your parents.

Imagine yourself as Mary. You're a poor mother with a newborn infant. You trusted your husband when he suddenly awoke from a restless dream that night in Bethlehem. You trusted as you fled the city of Bethlehem at night. You trusted when you embarked on this perilous journey across dangerous territory. You trusted when you were suddenly jumping into the dark unknown, unable to wait until the morning, when you could leave in the far safer company of the caravans. You trusted your husband. You trusted God.

Nazareth: School of the Ordinary

> What does me a lot of good when I think of the Holy Family is to imagine a life that was very ordinary. Little Jesus didn't perform useless miracles, even to please his mother. Why weren't they transported into Egypt by a miracle which would have been necessary and so easy for God? In the twinkling of an eye, they could have been brought there. No, everything in their life was done just as in our own. How many troubles, disappointments! How many times did others make complaints to good St. Joseph! How many times did they refuse to pay him for his work! Oh! How astonished we would be if we only knew how much they had to suffer![3]
>
> — St. Thérèse of Lisieux

The return to Nazareth is one of the Holy Family's most remarkable moments. After their arduous and terrifying exile, after the endless cascade of prophecies which foretold their existence from all time and were fulfilled in their midst, the Holy Family returns to the ordinary. A great hush descends on them. It's the great calm before the gathering storm, the peace before the final battle.

Saint José Manyanet, the "Apostle of the Holy Family," invites us to become, like Jesus, a child of Mary and Joseph, and enter into the School of Nazareth: "Let us imagine that we are there in the House of Nazareth in the company of our beloved parents Jesus, Mary and Joseph, listening to their words and observing their actions, and that with paternal affection they say to each one of us: If you want to please us, do not fail to copy in yourself what we say and do."[4]

What's the School of Nazareth? It's the place where we can simply abide with the Holy Family and learn every virtue from them. We learn to undertake all the ordinary — sometimes insufferably boring, sometimes unbearably grinding — aspects of our lives with the Holy Family. Nazareth is home to our daily martyrdom and our everyday joys.

As we discussed yesterday, in the School of Nazareth, we find great intimacy with the Holy Family in the ordinary and the everyday. Jesus, Mary, and Joseph performed the same workaday tasks you do. In prayer, we join them in their tasks, and they join us in ours. Bring the Holy Family to your dinner table. Work and play and eat with them. At the end of your day, rest with the Holy Family. Stay with them by offering your daily life as a prayer together with them.

No human being has ever been or will ever be holier than this husband and wife. And yet, these two souls didn't help Jesus in His preaching and teaching. Joseph's death would initiate the series of events that led to Jesus leaving Nazareth and beginning his public ministry. Also, Mary, as far as we know, remained quietly at home during almost all of Jesus' public life and ministry.

Mary and Joseph's offering to Jesus was the love of a father and mother in a true family. In turn, Jesus rendered to them the homage of a true son. The Holy House of Nazareth contained a great paradox. Could any lives have been more ordinary than those at Nazareth, yet were any lives holier?

Consecrate yourself to the Holy Family that your life too may be made holy.

Pray the Litany of the Holy Family *(page 207)*.

DAY 10

Jesus, Mary, and Joseph, Son, Mother, and Father of the Holy Family, have pity on us

> Wives, be subject to your husbands, as to the Lord. For the husband is the head of the wife as Christ is the head of the Church, his body, and is himself its Savior. As the Church is subject to Christ, so let wives also be subject in everything to their husbands. Husbands, love your wives, as Christ loved the Church and gave himself up for her, that he might sanctify her, having cleansed her by the washing of water with the word, that he might present the church to himself in splendor, without spot or wrinkle or any such thing, that she might be holy and without blemish. Even so, husbands should love their wives as their own bodies. He who loves his wife loves himself. For no man ever hates his own flesh, but nourishes and cherishes it, as Christ does the Church, because we are members of his body. "For this reason a man shall leave his father and mother and be joined to his wife, and the two shall become one flesh." This is a great mystery, and I mean in reference to Christ and the Church; however, let each one of you love his wife as himself, and let the wife see that she respects her husband.
>
> — Eph 5:22–33

Have you ever wondered who might have provided the model marriage described in Ephesians 5 above? Who modeled this for Jesus, that husbands are to give up their lives for their wives? It was St. Joseph. Many times, St. Joseph laid down his life in the service of his wife and the Holy Family. Also, who would have been the model husband and wife, not just for Jesus, but for the early Christian communities, as well, including St. Paul, the author of the Letter to the Ephesians? After all, St. Paul wrote this to the early Christians living in Ephesus. Who would have been the model mother and wife of the community in Ephesus? The Blessed Virgin Mary, of course! Jesus gave the Blessed Mother to St. John on the Cross when He said to him, "Behold, your Mother!" (Jn 19:27). Years later, St. John moved north with the Blessed Mother to Ephesus, and she was the most prominent member of the Christian community in Ephesus, along with the Apostle John.

Ephesians 5 tells us that wives are to be like the Church. What wife was the perfect model of the Church, the model *par excellence*? Again, the Virgin Mary. The mystical reality of the Church is deeply connected to the Virgin Mary. The Woman of Revelation 12, who is "clothed with the sun, with the moon under her feet, and on her head a crown of twelve stars" (Rev 12:1), is both Mary and the Church. Regarding her spiritual maternity, everything we can say about the Virgin Mary, we can say about the Church. Likewise, everything we can say about the Church, we can say about the Virgin Mary. The Church is also the image of our Immaculate Mother, who is holy "without spot or wrinkle or any such thing" and "without blemish."

These are deep spiritual realities to ponder. Take a moment to re-read Ephesians 5, but now think of the Holy Family, the holy marriage of Mary and Joseph, and the headship of St. Joseph.

The Dignity of Fatherhood

> Jesus and Mary not only bent their wills to Joseph's, for he was head of the Holy Family, but they lovingly surrendered their hearts to him as well.[1]
>
> — St. Peter Julian Eymard

> In Joseph, heads of the household are blessed with the unsurpassed model of fatherly watchfulness and care.[2]
>
> — Pope Leo XIII

Many today would bristle at calling a man — *any* man, even St. Joseph — the head of the family. Thankfully, God is not concerned with political correctness. God established the family. He appointed the father to be the head of the family, as an image of Himself as God the Father. This is the source of the immense dignity of fatherhood. Does this mean that men are better than women? No. The greatest human person who ever lived wasn't a man, but a woman: Mary, the Mother of God, the Immaculate Conception. Jesus is the greatest member of all mankind, but He is a Divine Person, having both a divine and human nature. Nevertheless, these two delighted in the headship of St. Joseph in their home. Saint Joseph was the head of the Holy House of Nazareth, even though he was far surpassed in dignity and holiness by everyone else in his house.

Why would people be so offended by this headship terminology these days? Why is this kind of male leadership often called toxic? Sadly, people are often offended by such language today because they have suffered emotional, physical, or even sexual abuse by father figures — fathers who misused their headship. This kind of abuse breaks God's Heart. It also breaks apart the family, sometimes many generations of families. What is needed to correct this is an example of virtuous and sacrificial fatherly leadership. Saint Joseph is the answer!

If men would imitate the head of the Holy Family and everyone would take St. Joseph as their own spiritual father, especially if our own fathers have fallen short, we would experience a renewal of family life and a return to honoring fatherhood and true masculinity. By looking to St. Joseph, we learn that the strength, authority, and headship of the father is given to him only to allow him to serve others.

The Greatness of Motherhood

If the dignity of fatherhood comes from becoming an image of God the Father, the greatness of motherhood comes from God's own Heart. Saint Thérèse of Lisieux said, "The loveliest masterpiece of the heart of God is the heart of a mother."[3] Regarding motherhood, Ven. Pope Pius XII wrote, "Through the pen of the Apostle, St. Paul, the Holy Spirit points out the greatness and joy of motherhood: God gives the child to the mother, but, together with the gift, he makes her cooperate effectively at the opening of the flower, of which he has deposited the germ in her womb, and this cooperation becomes a way which leads her to her eternal salvation."[4]

After mankind fell because of the actions of Adam and Eve, suffering entered the world. God punished men and women, and as a result they had to labor and toil in pain. It was a curse and a blessing, a remedy for the fall. God undertook to teach His wayward children the connection between love and suffering. This is especially true of the pain of childbirth and motherhood. Saint Paul tells us that "women will be saved through bearing children" (1 Tim 2:15). More than this, *all* mankind was saved through motherhood. It was through the childbearing of one woman, one singular woman who bears the title of motherhood itself: the Blessed Mother.

A strange thing happens to a woman when she delivers a child, an experience which connects the word "delivery" to "deliverance." Jesus explained this strange experience to His disciples in St. John's Gospel (the very apostle who received the Blessed Mother as his own mother: "When a woman is in labor, she has pain, because her hour has come, but when she is delivered of the child, she no longer remembers the anguish, for joy that a child is born into the world" [Jn 16:21]). Here Jesus unravels the mysterious joy of Easter. Our Lord endured such suffering when His hour had come, before the deliverance of Easter morning. He did this because of His great love for us. Then, in Jesus' glorious Resurrection, we are all born again as new sons and daughters of the Church. The suffering of Lent is forgotten as we bask in the triumph of Easter. The Easter deliverance is a New Exodus, a journey of faith, hope, and love. Easter prefigures the deliverance of all mankind, when all the sufferings of this world will be forgotten and replaced by eternal joy. In this day, there will be "a woman clothed with the sun," who is both the Blessed Mother and the Church, and she will cry out "in her pangs of birth, in anguish for delivery" (Rev 12:1–2). For, as St. Teresa Benedicta of the Cross explains, "To be a mother is to nourish and protect true humanity and bring it to development."[5] In this way, consecrating yourself to the Holy Family and Mary's motherhood, specifically, is essential for your spiritual development.

Children are a blessing!

Children are a very great blessing. They demonstrate the infinite fruitfulness of God. The Psalms tell us that the man who fears the Lord will be blessed with a wife "like a fruitful vine within [his] house" and children "like olive shoots around [his] table" (Ps 128:3–4). Unfortunately, many scoff at and deride this idea that children are a blessing, seeing children instead as a great burden or obstacle to personal success. But just read Isaiah's prophecy below and feel the great yearning that Israel experienced as it anticipated the birth of the long-awaited child, the Messiah:

> For to us a child is born,
> to us a son is given;
> and the government will be upon his shoulder,
> and his name will be called
> "Wonderful Counselor, Mighty God,
> Everlasting Father, Prince of Peace."
> Of the increase of his government and of peace
> there will be no end. (Is 9:6–7)

The pages of the Gospel reveal how special Christ's own love for children was. Pope St. Pius X wrote the following about Jesus: "It was his delight to be in their midst; He was wont to lay His hands on them; He embraced them; and He blessed them."[6] Jesus, in fact, grew angry when His disciples attempted to shoo the children away, and He rebuked them, saying, "Let the little children come to me, and do not hinder them; for to such belongs the kingdom of heaven" (Mt 19:14). Why does Jesus say this? Pope St. John Paul II provides us with the answer: "We must open our eyes to admire God Who hides and at the same time reveals Himself in things and introduces us into the realms of mystery ... we must be pure and simple like children, capable of admiring, being astonished, of marveling, and being enchanted by the divine gestures of love and closeness we witness."[7]

We see the image of God through the fruitfulness of children. We remember God through the astonishment of children. We see God hidden in the simple gifts of childhood. And, through consecration to the Holy Family, we become members of the household of God more fully.

Pray the Litany of the Holy Family (page 207).

DAY 11

Jesus, Mary, and Joseph, Divine Child, pure spouse, and chaste spouse, have pity on us

> To prayer must be added frequent and fervent use of the Sacrament of Penance which, as a spiritual medicine, purifies and heals us; likewise it is necessary to receive the Eucharist, which … is the best remedy against lust. The more pure and chaste is a soul, the more it hungers for this bread, from which it derives strength to resist all temptations to sins of impurity, and by which it is more intimately united with the Divine Spouse; "He who eats my flesh and drinks my blood, abides in me and I in him" (John 6:57). The eminent way to protect and nourish an unsullied and perfect chastity, as proven by experience time and again throughout the course of centuries, is solid and fervent devotion to the Virgin Mother of God … who is the Virgin of virgins and the "teacher of virginity."[1]
>
> — Venerable Pope Pius XII

The greatest teachers of virginity and chastity reside in the School of Nazareth. We consecrate ourselves to Mary and Joseph in order that their instruction may help us desire their Divine Son, Jesus, in the Eucharist more and more. When we consume the Eucharist, He who abides in the Holy House of Nazareth will abide in us, and we will abide in Him.

The Need for Chaste Men

"Blessed are the pure in heart, for they shall see God" (Mt 5:8). We need chaste men because the sins of lust blind men from seeing God. These sins also darken the intellect. Men become mindless and blind when they commit sins of impurity. We need chaste men because we need leaders and holy fathers. The devil would prefer to render all men mindless and blind. The pandemic of pornography and other offenses against the Sixth Commandment we are currently witnessing is the devil's campaign to destroy male leadership and the family in particular.

The devil is not hiding this fact. Pornography has been used in modern warfare multiple times as armies have used pornography to cripple and demoralize their enemies from within. In 2002, Israeli soldiers took the city of Ramallah in Palestine and gained control of three of the four TV stations in the city. They flooded the airwaves with pornography and effectively incapacitated the enemy.[2]

Saint Thomas Aquinas came from a wealthy family, and they did everything possible to oppose his vocation to be a Dominican. In an attempt to stop him from becoming a friar, his family brought him a prostitute, but he chased her out with a burning log.[3] From that day forward, he never suffered from lustful thoughts again. Without such thoughts harassing him, St. Thomas became one of the most prolific writers in history.

The irony of sins of lust, that is, misusing our sexual drive, is that they make men spiritually impotent. The devil is not threatened by impure men. They pose no opposition to his kingdom of darkness. Rather, what the devil greatly fears are chaste and pure men. They are a threat to all the enemies of light. Today the world needs such men as never before.

The Beauty of Modest Women

> The world does not need merely what women *have*, but rather what we are.[4]
>
> — St. Teresa Benedicta of the Cross

There is a story told about Bishop Nonnus of Edessa and St. Pelagia, a renowned actress and courtesan in 5th-century Antioch. When Pelagia passed by a group of bishops, all averted their eyes due to her immodest dress, except for

Bishop Nonnus. Pelagia smiled at the Bishop coyly and said, "Perhaps I am revealing too much?" Gazing upon her in compassion and sorrow for her lost soul, the Bishop responded, "No, perhaps you are revealing too little." This encounter profoundly affected Pelagia, leading to her conversion to Christianity and a life of penance.[5] The Bishop did not mean that she should have been more immodest. He was saying that the world needed her purity, not her impurity. The world needed the full beauty of what she was, not merely what allurements her body might have had.

The most beautiful woman the world has ever known was also the purest of all women. When the Virgin Mary appeared to the children of Fatima and La Salette, St. Bernadette in Lourdes, and St. Faustina in Poland, all the visionaries described her as being the most beautiful woman they had ever seen.[6] Sister Lucia dos Santos describes the first time they beheld Our Lady of Fatima: "We beheld a beautiful Lady all dressed in white. She was more brilliant than a crystal glass filled with sparkling water with the rays of the burning sun shining through it."[7]

Saint Francis de Sales calls modesty "the greatest ornament of beauty, and the best excuse for the want of it."[8] That is to say, one great, if imperfect, reason to desire modesty is to become beautiful. More importantly, the world needs to learn what beauty is, specifically what feminine beauty is and what it is not. What often passes for beauty today is a lie in the language of the body. The lie holds that true femininity is about wielding sexual and reproductive power, treating men as the oppressors of women, and clinging to youth through surgery and other means. Modern philosophy would have us reevaluate all truth in terms of power. The beauty of womanhood, however, is in its receptivity to life. This receptivity to life is necessarily modest, because a woman conceals all these miracles within her womb and, like the Virgin Mary, "[ponders] them in her heart" (Lk 2:19).

The Family is Pro-Life!

The family is, by its very nature, pro-life. The family conceives, protects, and nurtures life. This is what the family *does.* The family is pro-life because it reflects the image of the three Persons of the Holy Trinity. In the Holy Trinity, the love of two of the Divine Persons is so palpable that it is a third Person, the Holy Spirit, who proceeds eternally from the Father and the Son. The family reflects this when an entirely new person is created from the marital union of husband and wife.[9] If a family is not fruitful, biologically or otherwise, it fails to serve the end for which God created it. That's when bad things happen — bad things both inside the family and throughout the rest of society. Saint Teresa of Calcutta described this phenomenon: "We must not be surprised when we hear of murders, of killings, of wars, of hatred. If a mother can kill her own child, what is left but for us to kill each other?"[10]

"Amongst the blessings of marriage, the child holds the first place."[11] The Creator of the entire cosmos and the human race itself chose us as His helpers in the propagation of life. This is why His very first command to Adam and Eve was to "be fruitful and multiply, and fill the earth" (Gen 1:28). God said this at the time of the institution of marriage, which is the first and most critical of all human institutions. He said this to our first parents, and through them to all future parents and spouses. The command to be pro-life is the original commandment. It's written into the fabric of the entire human race, beginning in Eden and echoing through all generations.

It's the destiny of Christian parents to not only propagate the human race on earth, but to contribute to the growing number of saints in Heaven as well. Through the Holy Family, the infinite fruitfulness of the womb of Mary, and the waters of Baptism, parents not only give natural life, but raise their children to new life as saints.

Pray the Litany of the Holy Family (page 207).

DAY 12

Jesus, Mary, and Joseph, Restorers of Fallen Families, have pity on us

> Go to Joseph, the mender of broken toys, furniture, houses, as well as broken hearts, souls, bodies, minds, and families. Yes, let us go to Joseph, whom Jesus and Mary love so much.[1]
>
> — Servant of God Catherine Doherty

Satan is actively trying to destroy, not just families, but the institution of the family itself. We are rapidly approaching the point where more marriages fail than succeed. According to Venerable Sr. Lucia dos Santos of Fatima, "The final battle between the Lord and the kingdom of Satan will be about Marriage and the Family. ... Nevertheless, Our Lady has already crushed his head."[2] We may very well be in the midst of this "final confrontation," because the very definition of marriage is now under attack from multiple angles, including through the normalization of homosexual unions, contraception, abortion, and even divorce and adultery, among other corruptions. However the family will be restored if we go to Jesus, Mary, and Joseph.

The covenant of marriage can only occur between one man and one woman, precluding any homosexual unions. "Marriage" or "*matrimonium*" comes from the word "matrimony," which means motherhood. Marriage, by its very nature, is ordered to conception, not contraception. Moreover, the covenant of marriage is only completed when the spouses come together in the marital union. This means the spouses are not husband and wife until they form a sexual union with the desire that children should come from this union.[3] Children may or may not come from the sexual union of spouses, but the covenant is perfected by this intention.

God is a Trinity, a union of persons so fruitful that a third Person proceeds eternally therefrom. This outpouring of life is essential to God's nature, and so it's essential to the nature of marriage and the family. This unceasing fruitfulness, not any form of population control, is fundamental to God's plan. God's instructions from the beginning were to "be fruitful and multiply, and fill the earth" (Gen 1:28). This was a command and a promise. This promise is fulfilled in the infinite fruitfulness of the Holy Family. The union of Mary and Joseph, though celibate and virginal, is nevertheless infinitely fruitful. For it's through this union that we can all be made brothers and sisters of Christ. Through the Holy Family, mankind at last fulfills this command and its promise by filling the entire earth. Through the Holy Family as well, God's family will prevail in this "final battle ... over Marriage and the Family."[4]

Fallen Families

The first fallen family to be restored by the Holy Family was their own: the family of King David, whose family tree had become just a stump, the "stump of Jesse." Saint Joseph is "of the House of David" (Lk 1:27).

At the time of Christ, the house of David and the entire Kingdom of Israel had fallen on very difficult times. The Northern Kingdom, which was originally composed of 10 of the tribes of Israel, had been conquered, ransacked, and taken captive by the Assyrian Empire. This is the origin of the so-called "Lost Tribes" of Israel. The Southern Kingdom, which was composed of the remaining two tribes, Judah and Benjamin, had likewise been conquered by the Babylonian Empire later. The line of Davidic kings had fallen. That family tree had been cut down. It was now only the "stump of Jesse," David's father (Is 11:1). But the prophets repeated again and again that a branch would shoot forth from the stump of Jesse, as we have discussed. One of the last surviving seeds of this once-great royal family which had not been scattered was St. Joseph. He was the hidden King of Israel. His claim to the throne of David and the kingship of Israel was one of the best in all Israel.

It's hard to imagine a family falling further, or rising higher, than King David's family. The world and its empires had done all it could to stamp out David's line. The family of David, too, had done all it could to destroy the family on its own. You don't have to read much of the writings of the prophets Jeremiah and Isaiah to learn about the terrible idolatry and adultery committed by David's descendants. As Jeremiah said, "You have played the harlot with many lovers; and would you return to me? says the Lord … Where have you not been lain with?" (Jer 3:1–2). And yet, the earthly crown of David remains. It was passed down to St. Joseph, who could then pass it to the King of Kings. Jesus restores the Kingdom of Israel, bringing together not just the tribe of Judah, but all the tribes and even all mankind. Jesus gathers them all, leading them to the ultimate Promised Land, the Kingdom of Heaven.

If you think the Holy Family can restore the broken and pitiful family of David but can't help you or your family, you're wrong. There is no amount of sin — adultery, idolatry, abuse, even murder — that the Holy Family hasn't already overcome. As the hymn says, "Through many dangers, toils, and snares, we have already come," and "grace will lead us home." The Holy Family is our home, the home of Jesus and the unshakeable, unfallen home of all mankind. No family is lost that can still reach out for the Holy Family.

Marital Struggles

> Don't say, "That person bothers me." Think: "That person sanctifies me."[5]
>
> — St. Josemaría Escrivá

The Sacrament of Marriage is such that every moment of it can be used to draw the spouses closer to one another and to

Heaven simultaneously. This goes for all the aggravations of married life, as well as all of its graces. This certainly includes all the struggles of marriage, of which there can be many which go far beyond toilet-seat and toothpaste tube issues to financial hardship, religious conflicts, and even adultery and divorce. G. K. Chesterton describes the struggle this way: "Marriage is a duel to the death, which no man of honour should decline."[6] To extend the metaphor, marriage with children is execution by firing squad. It's the execution, we hope, of all our vices and vanities through sanctification. Among the greatest of marital struggles, of course, is the opposite kind of suffering: infertility or even the loss of children.

To understand God's plan for marriage in the midst of childlessness, we turn again to St. Josemaría Escrivá: "God in his providence has two ways of blessing marriages: one by giving them children; and the other, sometimes, because he loves them so much, by not giving them children. I don't know which is the better blessing."[7] He is not suggesting that childlessness is a blessing because the spouses are free to travel the world or pursue their own interests. Rather, he is pointing out that the intense desire for children can bring spouses closer together and closer to Jesus together.

God draws spouses to Himself through their grief or longing. Saint Teresa of Calcutta also described this: "Remember pain, sorrow, suffering are but the kiss of Jesus — a sign that you have come so close to him that he can kiss you."[8]

The Holy Family wants to comfort spouses in their struggles. They were surely no strangers to death and grief. Simeon prophesied to Mary, "[A] sword will pierce through your own soul" (Lk 2:35). Mary and Joseph knew from Simeon's prophecy that their Son would suffer. They learned something else from it, too, something that must have broken St. Joseph's Heart. They learned that St. Joseph would die before the hour of Jesus' suffering. Saint Joseph would not be there to comfort his Son or his wife, or else a sword would have surely pierced his Heart as well. The pain of losing their child was, therefore, always before Mary and Joseph. And yet, the Holy House of Nazareth overflowed with joy. The Holy Family welcomes you into their home, where sorrow is turned into joy, the joy of being so close to Jesus that He can kiss you.

Sacrificial Love

We are willing to bend over backwards for our families, unless, of course, it requires sacrifice. Saint Teresa of Calcutta describes this paradox: "It is easy to love the people far away. It is not always easy to love those close to us."[9] Often, we can't reach far enough to touch those closest to us, and it's those we love and know best who elude us. The institution of the family is either the most well-tailored torture device or the school of sacrificial love.

The Holy Family can teach you how to deal with this paradox of closeness within the family. Mary and Joseph, the greatest saints of all, were utterly powerless to prevent Jesus' suffering. Jesus is closer to us than we are to ourselves, and He was even closer to Mary and Joseph, but Mary couldn't reach out and stop any of His suffering. Saint Joseph was able to protect Jesus and Mary from the worst suffering, but only for a time. Even he knew that a time was approaching when he, too, would be powerless to stop the evil coming for his family.

Herein lies the intense sorrow of the Holy Family, of Our Lady of Sorrows and St. Joseph, the Prince of Sorrows. We can place all our sufferings at the foot of the Cross, and Jesus will bear them all away. This is His great gift to us. But what about Mary and Joseph? Could they pass on their suffering for their own child to their own child? Could you? Imagine that. This is a deep mystery of the human spirit, but yes, even they, Mary and Joseph, could lay their suffering at the foot of the Cross. In fact, they show us how.

Jesus taking away their suffering was in itself a kind of sacrifice offered up by Mary and Joseph, since parents desire to take away their children's suffering. This is why Pope St. John Paul II said, "Prayer joined to sacrifice constitutes the most powerful force in human history."[10] Combining prayer and sacrifice, as St. Paul says, is "heaping burning coals on the heads" of those who commit crimes and injustices, in order to right these injustices (see also Rom 12:20). Prayer and sacrifice are "sharper than any two-edged sword, piercing to the division of soul and spirit, of joints and marrow, and discerning the thoughts and intentions of the heart" (Heb 4:12).

Prayer and sacrifice are the way to achieve intimacy with Jesus. What two people in history spent more of their lives in face-to-face intimacy with Jesus? Who kissed Jesus' precious face more than these two? So close was she that Mary's last kisses were blood-stained. And who in human history, after Jesus Himself, have sacrificed more than Mary and Joseph, who sacrificed Jesus, their own Son? The institution of the family is the foundation of God's plan for salvation, the foundation of the Church itself. It's, therefore, the most important institution in human history. For this reason, the Holy Family, as a restorer of fallen families and the greatest union of prayer and sacrifice, is the most powerful force in human history.

The Holy Family was separated once when Mary and Joseph lost the boy Jesus for three days in the Temple. This was a sort of preparation for the time when Mary would lose Jesus again for three days — when they would be separated by His death. The Holy Family was and is the closest of all families. Because of this closeness, the separation they experienced at Jesus' death, especially such a grotesque death, was one of the most painful separations imaginable.

This is why the Church holds two pious traditions. First, pious tradition maintains that the first person Jesus encountered among the dead was St. Joseph. Thus, not long after Christ's death, Son and father were reunited. Second, it holds that the first person Jesus appeared to after the Resurrection was His mother.

Death was ultimately powerless to separate the Holy Family. The Holy Family will draw your family closer and help prevent death from separating you from your loved ones, too.

Pray the Litany of the Holy Family (page 207).

DAY 13

Jesus, Mary, and Joseph, Image of the Blessed Trinity here on earth, have pity on us

> God had chosen to reveal himself by being born into a human family and the human family thus became an icon of God! God is the Trinity, he is a communion of love; so is the family despite all the differences that exist between the Mystery of God and his human creature, an expression that reflects the unfathomable Mystery of God as Love. In marriage the man and the woman, created in God's image, become "one flesh" (Gen 2: 24), that is a communion of love that generates new life. The human family, in a certain sense, is an icon of the Trinity because of its interpersonal love and the fruitfulness of this love.[1]
>
> — Pope Benedict XVI

God created us. He knows our need to see — at least with our mind's eye —– in order to know, and to know in order to love. But the Holy Trinity, which is ineffable, can't be reduced to an image. Nevertheless, God found a way to reveal Himself to us. He reveals Himself to us through the Holy Family. The family, specifically the Holy Family, is an insight into the very nature of God. That insight is fruitfulness through an intimate union. The Holy Trinity is infinitely fruitful. Everything in the cosmos is the fruit of the Trinity. How could any family, no matter its size, ever be *that* fruitful?

All mankind descends from the original Holy Family, the family of Adam and Eve, who fell. From the family of Abraham and Sarah, though "as good as dead, were born descendants as many as the stars of Heaven and as the innumerable grains of sand by the seashore" (Heb 11:12). These families, who became the largest of all through natural propagation, are still surpassed in fruitfulness by Mary and Joseph, who became the parents of all mankind through Mary's virginal womb.

JMJ: The Earthly Trinity

The Liturgy for the Feast of the Holy Family presents the familiar Gospel episode of the 12-year-old Jesus who stays behind in the Temple in Jerusalem without His parents' knowledge. Mary and Joseph, surprised and anxious, discover Him three days later conversing with the teachers. Jesus answers His mother that He "must be in His Father's house," that is, God's house (Lk 2:49). The Temple was, or at least had been, the abiding place of the Holy Trinity on earth. It had been home to the Ark of the Covenant, the Glory Cloud, and other manifestations of the power of God the Father, such as the smiting of Zechariah, narrated just a chapter earlier in Luke. Jesus appears somewhat surprised that His mother would ask Him to explain His presence in the Temple. Surely, she must know that His home is not the Temple, per se, but the Holy Trinity. How could Jesus be anywhere else? Jesus might leave the Temple, but He never leaves the Holy Trinity.

The point is not that Jesus chooses one trinity over the other. Rather when He chooses to return to Nazareth, He is choosing to connect the earthly trinity to the Holy Trinity.

Image and Imitation

God does nothing without purpose. His decision to reveal Himself to us through the family is not an exercise in vanity. He is reaching out to us — always reaching. God draws us to Himself through His image. When it reflects the image of the Holy Trinity, the family is the path to encounter and know God. Pope Benedict XVI explains the true meaning of the Feast of the Holy Family:

> Having come into the world, into the heart of a family, God shows that this institution is a sure path on which to encounter and come to know him, as well as an ongoing call to work for the unity of all people centered on love. Hence one of the greatest services that we Christians can render our fellow human beings is to offer them our serene and unhesitating witness as a family founded on the marriage of a man and a woman, safeguarding and promoting the family, since it is of supreme importance for the present and future of humanity.[2]

The witness of the family is "one of the greatest services" that we can render to the human family. Be a great family member. Whether it's your blood family, your Christian family, or the human family, love, serve, and sacrifice for them and protect the institution of the family. For the sake of humanity's future, we must reflect the grace of the Holy Trinity to the world. But how do we reflect what is ineffable? How do we imitate what is inimitable? This is why Jesus was born to us: "For to us a child is born, to us a son is given" (Is 9:6).

The Holy Family, the earthly trinity, is the best image of the Holy Trinity. It's, therefore, the best path to encounter and know God. The members of the Holy Family are our bridge to the Holy Trinity. They teach us the true meaning of family, and family teaches us the nature of God. Our serene and unhesitating witness as a family is our imitation of the Holy Family. Reach out to the Holy Family so that they may draw you closer to the Holy Trinity. Imitate the virtues of the Holy Family so that you may illuminate the world.

The Triumph of the Family

The defeat of the family represents the defeat of God's plan for mankind. It means the end of the message of salvation. We need only look around to see the defeat of the family.

Divorce, abortion, human trafficking, contraception — the human family is trying to coexist with these toxins, trying to grow despite these pollutions. It's growing warped and perverse. Just take the specter of transhumanism for example — does anybody know where the human family's parents are? Fertility rates are collapsing. The family is becoming sterile, and it'll soon be dead, long before it hits the ground. The defeat of the family means extinction or worse.

If this is what the defeat of the family looks like, what would the triumph of the family look like? To understand its triumph, we need to first understand its mission. Pope Benedict XVI answers this for us as well:

> Indeed, the family is the best school at which to learn to live out those values which give dignity to the person and greatness to peoples. In the family sorrows and joys are shared, since all feel enveloped in the love that prevails at home, a love that stems from the mere fact of belonging to the same family. I ask God that in your homes you may always breathe this love of total self-giving and faithfulness which Jesus brought to the world with his birth, nurturing and strengthening it with daily prayer, the constant practice of the virtues, reciprocal understanding and mutual respect. I then encourage you so that, trusting in the motherly intercession of Mary Most Holy, Queen of Families, and under the powerful protection of St Joseph, her spouse, you may dedicate yourselves tirelessly to this beautiful mission which the Lord has placed in your hands.[3]

May Jesus, Mary, and Joseph envelop us in the love that prevailed in their home. May they lead all peoples to their family, the common destination of all mankind. May they help us to know the love that stems from all belonging to the same family, the Holy Family. This would be the ultimate triumph of the family, the adoption of all people into the Holy Family. This is the mission of the family. The method is described in Pope Benedict XVI's prayer for our homes: (1) to always breathe this love of total self-giving and faithfulness, (2) to be nurtured and strengthened with daily prayer, and (3) to constantly practice the virtues and demonstrate reciprocal understanding and mutual respect.

Pray the Litany of the Holy Family (page 207).

DAY 14

Holy Family, tested by the greatest of difficulties, have pity on us

> Understand, rest very much assured, my youngest child, that nothing whatsoever should frighten you or worry you. Do not be troubled or weighed down with grief. Do not fear any illness or vexation, anxiety or pain. Am I not here who am your Mother? Are you not under my shadow and protection? Am I not your fountain of life? Are you not in the folds of my mantle? In the crossing of my arms? Is there anything else you need? Do not let anything worry you or upset you further. Do not let your uncle's illness worry you, for he will not die of what he now has. Rest assured, for he has already recovered.[1]
>
> — Our Lady of Guadalupe to St. Juan Diego

With Our Lady as your spiritual mother, what do you need to fear? The Holy Family, your family, has been tested by the greatest difficulties. Despite this, the Holy Family not only survived but prospered. You are under their protection and have nothing to be worried about.

The first Holy Family of Adam and Eve fell because of the temptations of the devil. Eve, then Adam, experienced three different temptations: "So when the woman saw that the tree was [1] good for food, and that it was [2] a delight to the eyes, and that the tree was [3] to be desired to make one wise, she took of its fruit and ate; and she also gave some to her husband, and he ate" (Gen 3:6). These are called the "three-fold lusts" or "three-fold concupiscences": (1) the lust of the flesh, (2) the lust of the eyes, and (3) the pride of life (1 Jn 2:16). Original sin wounded human nature, and these three lusts are like the scar that remains.

Satan uses the same three-fold strategy on us again and again. Think about how most of our temptations fit into these three categories. These three temptations also correspond to Jesus' three temptations in the desert.

The Temptations of the World

In the Gospel accounts, the temptations of Jesus in the desert always immediately follow His Baptism. Why would events happen in this sequence? Why would the devil tempt Jesus immediately after His Baptism?

Jesus' Baptism was not a typical Baptism. For one, Jesus did not need to be cleansed of original sin, or any sin for that matter. What, then, was the purpose of Jesus' Baptism? Saint John the Baptist asked this exact question. He even attempted to forgo the honor of baptizing Jesus: "John would have prevented him, saying, 'I need to be baptized by you, and do you come to me?'" (Mt 3:14). Jesus' answer to John's question is a bit mysterious: "Let it be so now; for thus it is fitting for us to fulfil all righteousness" (Mt 3:15). Why is "all righteousness fulfilled" by John's Baptism of Jesus? Because this Baptism is an anointing. It's an anointing because it's a coronation. Jesus is receiving the earthly crown of Israel by anointing. The Hebrew word for "anointing" is Messiah; the Greek word is Christ. Jesus is being anointed on the crown of His head by a Levitical priest, St. John, which is the precise manner in which the kings of Israel were crowned. The next question you may be asking is: Where did Jesus' crown come from? This will answer why all this is happening in this particular sequence.

Where does a king's crown come from? In Israel, like most kingdoms in history, the crown was inherited and passed from father to son. Jesus' Heavenly Father is the King of Kings, but Jesus will not ascend to that throne until the Ascension. Jesus' earthly father, though crownless, gave to his adopted Son the legal title and ancestral rights of kingship that had been passed down to him, from generation after generation all the way from King David. For the son to inherit the crown, however, the father must die. This means that a certain event had to occur to put all these other events in motion: the death of St. Joseph.

Satan knows that Jesus is the Messiah. Jesus' public ministry has now officially begun. Listen now to Satan's third temptation of Jesus. Satan tempts Jesus with more crowns and kingdoms, with power, which is the third lust, "pride of life":

> Again, the devil took him to a very high mountain, and showed him all the kingdoms of the world and the glory of them; and he said to him, "All these I will give you, if you will fall down and worship me." Then Jesus said to him, "Begone, Satan! for it is written, 'You shall worship the Lord your God, and him only shall you serve.'" Then the devil left him, and behold, angels came and ministered to him. (Mt 4:8–11)

Jesus was shown how to wear the earthly crown by His father, St. Joseph, who wore the crown as a mantle of humility. Following his example, Jesus wore the diadem of royalty as a crown of thorns. The Holy Family is a royal family. Through them, we are heirs to all the world and Heaven as well. Also, the Holy Family protects us from the temptations of Satan and conceals us from him. The Holy Family dethrones Satan as the ruler of this world and claims you as their own.

The Temptations of the Flesh

Satan also tempts Jesus with the "lust of the flesh." Just as Adam and Eve "saw that the tree was good for food" (Gen 3:6), Satan tempts Jesus to turn stones into bread. Adam and Eve fell to the allure of the fruit of the tree of knowledge of good and evil, despite being surrounded by an orchard of the most beautiful, most perfect fruits imaginable. Adam and Eve's bellies and all their needs were already fully satisfied by God, and yet they fell. Jesus had just finished fasting for 40 days! In one of the greatest understatements of the Bible, we are told that "afterward he was hungry." Can you imagine how hungry Jesus would have been? And yet, He doesn't succumb to Satan tempting Him with food. Here's the account of Satan's temptation of Jesus:

> Jesus was led up by the Spirit into the wilderness to be tempted by the devil. And he fasted forty days and forty nights, and afterward he was hungry. And the tempter came and said to him, "If you are the Son of God, command these stones to become loaves of bread." But he answered, "It is written, 'Man shall not live by bread alone, but by every word that proceeds from the mouth of God.'" (Mt 4:1–4)

Satan attempts to goad the newly crowned King of Israel, addressing Him by the title used for the kings of Israel: "Son of God." Jesus responds to Satan's attack with the Word of God, for Jesus *is* the Word of God. He responds by citing Deuteronomy. Here is the full verse: "[God] humbled you and let you hunger and fed you with manna, which you did not know, nor did your fathers know; that he might make you know that man does not live by bread alone but that man lives by every word that proceeds out of the mouth of the Lord" (8:3). Jesus is telling Satan about the manna which came down from Heaven. Jesus is the manna which came down from Heaven. Not only that, the New Manna, the Eucharist, is going to destroy Satan's reign of death.

Think about how well acquainted the Holy Family was with the Word of God. Mary gave birth to the Word of God. The Word of God was a living, breathing person in their home. He was a member of their family. Through the Holy Family, the Word of God will become part of your home and your family. You will be thoroughly armed against Satan's temptations with the sword of truth, the Word of God. The Holy Family will guide you through the greatest difficulties.

The Temptations of the Devil

Though the devil is crafty and cunning, he is repetitious. He continues to attack us using the same three tactics he has used from the beginning. Whatever same-old temptation the devil may throw at you, or whatever new spin on an old temptation you might encounter, go to the Holy Family. In difficulties of all sorts, go to the Holy Family. Mary and Joseph will always guide you to Jesus. They will always answer — in one way or another — every petition addressed to them. Have confidence in this statement. The Church holds this as a certainty. This is so certain that the Church has approved and granted indulgences for the prayer of St. Bernard of Clairvaux, which tells us exactly this, to go to Mary in all our difficulties. This is the *Memorare* prayer, so named for its first word in Latin:

> Remember, O most gracious Virgin Mary, that never was it known that anyone who fled to thy protection, implored thy help, or sought thy intercession was left unaided. Inspired with this confidence I fly unto thee, O Virgin of virgins, my mother. To thee I come, before thee I stand, sinful and sorrowful. O Mother of the Word Incarnate, despise not my petitions, but in thy mercy hear and answer me. Amen.

In times of the greatest difficulty, St. Teresa of Calcutta would pray what she called the "emergency novena." Her emergency novena is very simple. It's the *Memorare* prayed nine times in a row.

Not only is there a *Memorare* prayer to Mary, there is also one to Joseph. Many great saints have championed the merits of this prayer, including St. Faustina, who mentioned in her *Diary* that she prayed it every day and that St. Joseph himself told her to do so. It's a similar prayer and also begins with the word "remember":

> Remember, O most amiable, most benevolent, most kind, and most merciful father, St. Joseph, that the great St. Teresa [of Ávila] assures us that she never had recourse to thy protection without obtaining relief. Animated with this same confidence, O dear St. Joseph, I come to thee and groaning under the heavy burden of my many sins, I prostrate myself at your feet. O most compassionate father, do not, I beseech thee, reject my poor and miserable prayers, but graciously hear and obtain my petitions. Amen.

Go to the Holy Family in your times of greatest difficulty. Fly to them, as the angels fly to their Queen, the Virgin Mary. They will rescue you, as St. Joseph rescued the Holy Family from the Slaughter of the Innocents. Remember in your times of greatest difficulty that Mary and Joseph will always take you to their Son, who has already overcome all of Satan's temptations. As Our Lady of Guadalupe instructed St. Juan Diego, "Do not let anything worry you or upset you." Is the Holy Family not here, who is your family, your mother, father, and brother? Are you not under their shadow and protection? Are you not hidden within the folds of Mary's mantle and the cloak of St. Joseph? Is there not everything you need in their Divine Son, Jesus?

*Pray the Litany of the Holy Family (**page 207**).*

DAY 15

Holy Family, with much suffering on the journey to Bethlehem, have pity on us

> Looking today at that Holy House [of Nazareth], our thoughts turn *to the many families* of our time *who are in difficult situations.* … And what can be said *of the many attacks on the family institution itself?* All this shows how urgent it is to rediscover the value of the family and to help it in every way to be, as God wanted it, the vital environment where every child who comes into the world *is welcomed with tenderness and gratitude from the moment of his conception*; a place marked by a serene atmosphere that encourages the harmonious human and spiritual development of all its members.[1]
>
> — Pope St. John Paul II

Saint Joseph's ancestral home was Bethlehem, "the City of David," because his ancestor was King David. When David was just a boy, he was called to fight Goliath. When he was called, he was tending "his father's sheep at Bethlehem" (1 Sam 17:15). Not only was Bethlehem the home of David, David was also a shepherd of Bethlehem — more to come on this later.

Bethlehem was about 80 miles south of Nazareth. At the time of Jesus' birth, it was a hamlet with a population of no more than 2,000 people, a rural place. The journey from Nazareth to Bethlehem would have taken about three days under optimal conditions — but journeying with a woman in the ninth month of her pregnancy in winter was not optimal. Mary rode on a donkey while Joseph walked alongside, leading the animal. They likely had no servant to help them up and over the hills and rocky ground. The road first descended into the Plain of Esdraelon that separates the hills of Galilee from Samaria. Then, the road began to rise more and more into the "hill country of Judah," passing through frequent towns that alternated with farm country. Finally, about five or six miles south of Jerusalem, the two travelers reached their journey's end. Despite the suffering that the Holy Family endured, they persevered to the end of the journey. We can call on the Holy Family to help us through the long journeys of our own lives, to be with us step-by-step as we climb the hills and mountains of pain and suffering.

In Good Times and in Bad

Mary and Joseph were not afforded much of a honeymoon following their marriage. Their forced journey to Bethlehem was no vacation. It was an arduous journey undertaken during a very difficult time: the ninth month of Mary's pregnancy. And speaking of King David, he once journeyed along much the same path to Bethlehem as the Holy Family did. Not only that, but King David also journeyed with the Ark of the Covenant, just as his descendant, Joseph, now travels with the New Ark of the Covenant, the Blessed Virgin Mary. There is a stark contrast, however, between King David's riches and the Holy Family's poverty, between his triumphant procession and their forced journey, and finally between his treatment of the Ark and St. Joseph's reverence for it. David's journey with the Ark was marked by misfortune because of his irreverent treatment of it. These incidents prefigured the Holy Family's difficult journey to Bethlehem with the New Ark.

Only Levitical priests[2] were allowed to carry the Ark, and only then on poles — never actually touching it. However, during David's journey, the Levitical priests were not carrying the Ark. It had been placed on a cart and was being pulled by oxen instead (2 Sam 6:3). Oxen are a far cry from priests. Because of this irreverent treatment, the Ark began to tip and fall from the cart when the oxen stumbled. Seeing this, one of the Levitical priests in the Ark's procession, Uzzah, tried to stop it from falling. Uzzah "put out his hand to the Ark of God and took hold of it" (2 Sam 6:6). You might see this as a noble action, but touching the Ark was the exact action that God had strictly and specifically forbidden Uzzah's entire family branch of Levites from doing. It was the last straw. God smote Uzzah. Why did God do this? Despite all the riches of the king's procession, they were failing to give due reverence to the Ark of God.

Now think about the Holy Family taking nearly the same path through Judea. In the first days of her pregnancy, when Mary had visited Elizabeth, she had even passed very near the spot where Uzzah had been smote.[3] Despite the poverty of the Holy Family, St. Joseph doesn't fail to reverence the New Ark of God. Rather than oxen, Mary is riding atop another beast of burden, the donkey. Joseph, the descendant of King David, is again leading the procession. Mary, and Jesus within her womb, should have been borne up on the shoulders of priests with the greatest reverence, but "the world knew him not" (Jn 1:10), and the donkey was the best that a humble carpenter from Nazareth could afford. And yet, St. Joseph doesn't let the Blessed Mother, the New Ark, fall. He would have carried her himself, if he could have. Joseph is the priestly servant of the Ark that Uzzah failed to be. Together, Mary and Joseph are the perfect portrait of sacrificial love: Joseph enduring the physical difficulties of the journey to carry his family, and Mary enduring the discomforts of traveling while pregnant.

In Riches and in Poverty

King David's procession with the Ark to Jerusalem did not end with it being placed in a Temple. There was no palace waiting for the Ark of God, just a tent, just as there was "no place … in the inn" for Mary, the New Ark of God, just a stable (Lk 2:7). David was uncomfortable that he dwelt in a palace, while the Ark of God still dwelt in a tent. He promised to build a great temple as a home for the Ark, but God prevented him, saying that He would build a house for King David instead:

> [T]he Lord declares to you that the Lord will make you a house. When your days are fulfilled and you lie down with your fathers, I will raise up your offspring after you, who shall come forth from your body, and I will establish his kingdom. He shall build a house for my name, and I will establish the throne of his kingdom for ever. I will be his father, and he shall be my son. … And your house and your kingdom shall be made sure for ever before me; your throne shall be established for ever. (2 Sam 7:11–14, 16)

These words above from Nathan the prophet describe both Solomon, David's immediate son and heir, and the coming Messiah, Jesus. Even though the Kingdom of David will fall, God will restore this royal family through the Holy Family. Through them, David's "throne shall be established for ever." God will raise up the fallen family of David with a New David and a New Ark, but, like the Old Ark, the Holy Family will be given only the barest shelter at the end of their journey to Bethlehem. The contrast between King David's riches and the Holy Family's poverty is stark. They are the richest of all families, and yet abide in poverty, even squalor, for the birth of the King of Kings. According to God's design, however, their poverty illuminates these riches.

In Health and in Sickness

The prophecy that the Messiah will be born in Bethlehem connects the Blessed Mother to another mother; the pregnancies of these two mothers are a striking contrast of health and sickness. When the wise men came to King Herod, he assembled "all the chief priests and scribes of the people" and "inquired of them where the Christ was to be born" (Mt

2:4). They answered, "In Bethlehem of Judea" (Mt 2:5). To support this answer, they cited the prophecy of Micah:

> But you, O Bethlehem Ephrathah, who are little to be among the clans of Judah, from you shall come forth for me one who is to be ruler in Israel, whose origin is from of old, from ancient days … until the time when she who is in travail has brought forth; then the rest of his brethren shall return to the people of Israel. (Mic 5:2–3)

Note that the prophecy states "Bethlehem Ephrathah," not just Bethlehem. This is because the new matriarch of Israel is to give birth where the old matriarch of Israel gave birth and died. The phrase "she who is in travail" points both backward to Rachel and forward to Mary. According to Genesis, it was at Bethlehem-Ephrathah, the place between the two cities, where Rachel and Jacob had to take shelter when she suddenly went into "hard labor":

> Then they journeyed from Bethel; and when they were still some distance from Ephrath, Rachel travailed, and she had hard labor. And when she was in her hard labor, the midwife said to her, "Fear not; for now you will have another son." And as her soul was departing (for she died), she called his name Ben-oni [meaning "child of affliction" or "child of poverty"]; but his father called his name Benjamin. So Rachel died, and she was buried on the way to Ephrath (that is, Bethlehem), and Jacob set up a pillar upon her grave; it is the pillar of Rachel's tomb, which is there to this day. (Gen 35:16–20)

The two holy families of Mary and Rachel are connected in so many ways. Look at the name that Rachel originally chose for her son: Ben-oni, meaning "child of affliction" or "child of poverty." Though the health of Mary's pregnancy contrasts with Rachel's sickness, Rachel's hard labor and death point to the Holy Family's poverty, especially Jesus as the Suffering Servant,[4] and Mary as "Our Lady of Sorrows." Returning to the Gospel of Matthew, Rachel is mentioned again in reference to Herod's response to the visit by the wise men, the Slaughter of the Innocents: "A voice was heard in Ramah, wailing and loud lamentation, Rachel weeping for her children" (Mt 2:18).

Ever since Jacob "set up a pillar upon her grave," described above, the Jews have been visiting the tomb of Rachel, called "Kever Rachel" today. Just as we ask for the intercession of "Our Lady of Sorrows," the Jews have been praying for their holy mother, Rachel, to intercede for them before the heavenly throne for 3,000 years! The Jews even tell the story that, when the Babylonian army had conquered Israel and destroyed the Temple, as the Jewish survivors were being marched to Babylon in chains, they stopped to pray at Rachel's grave. All the patriarchs appeared before God at this time to pray for God to forgive their children, and Rachel found herself last in line behind Abraham, Isaac, Moses, and even her own husband, Jacob. God rejected all their prayers, but He couldn't refuse the tears of the mother. Now, God has given us a still greater pair of intercessors, the Holy Spouses, the mother and father of Jesus. Go to them in good times and bad, in riches and poverty, and in health and sickness.

Pray the Litany of the Holy Family (page 207)

DAY 16

Holy Family, without a welcome in Bethlehem, have pity on us

> There are two births of Christ, one unto the world in Bethlehem; the other in the soul, when it is spiritually reborn. Men think of the former much more than the later, and celebrate it every year; but the spiritual Bethlehem is equally momentous … It was the second birth that Saint Paul insisted on when he wrote from prison to his beloved people, the Ephesians, asking that Christ may dwell in their hearts by faith and that they be rooted and grounded in love. This is the second Bethlehem, or the personal relationship of the individual heart to the Lord Christ.[1]
>
> — Venerable Fulton J. Sheen

Why would the Holy Family not be welcome in Bethlehem? First, because, more often than not, we don't welcome Jesus into our hearts. This is the second Bethlehem that Venerable Fulton Sheen describes above. Second, the fact that there would be no welcome and "no room in the inn" (Lk 2:7) for the New Ark, Mary, was prefigured by the fact that the Old Ark still dwelt in a tent, not a palace or temple, at the end of King David's journey to Bethlehem. It wasn't right that Bethlehem received the Holy Family so poorly. It's still not right that the heart of man so often rejects Jesus. It was wrong for the "City of David" to reject the highest-ranking heirs of King David. It's still wrong for the world to reject its Ruler. These rejections are such a stark contrast to the way the Holy Family welcomes us — even *adopts* us — into their own family.

We have come to love our Christmas Nativity scenes with the manger set in the cave. Saint Francis of Assisi was, of course, right to begin this tradition. And yet, it should remain shocking to us that Mary, the most blessed woman of all creation, should have to deliver her baby in such squalor. There are rich spiritual truths to be learned from the Holy Family's poverty in the stable. It's to be hoped that we are reminded that the Nativity scene is not just a quaint, sentimental ornament that decorates our homes during Advent and Christmas. The Holy Family is the foundation of all homes, the new beginning of the entire human story. Let's now begin to unpack the spiritual mysteries contained deep within the cave.

Abandonment to Divine Providence

> She who knew better than anyone how to wait attentively for the Lord guides us and shows us how to make more vital and active our journey to the Holy Night of Bethlehem.[2]
>
> — Pope St. John Paul II

When we participate in the work of God's creation, we are partnering with the One who bears away mountains and builds civilizations with just a thought. The Holy Family, the greatest of God's partners, teaches us how to abandon ourselves to the Lord's plans, to His providence. Their journey to Bethlehem and final destination, the cave, is one of relentless abandonment to and trust in God's Will. But it wasn't passive. It was active abandonment. With each cold, hardscrabble step, the members of the Holy Family were throwing themselves into God's hands. Despite having these great teachers, however, such abandonment is not a lesson we easily learn. It's a grace that must be received to be even accepted. In the classic work, *Abandonment to Divine Providence*, Fr. Jean-Pierre de Caussade writes, "There is not a moment in which God does not present himself under the cover of some pain to be endured, of some consolation to be enjoyed, or of some duty to be performed."[3] This is the underlying message of the Holy Family's journey to Bethlehem. Every step is a mix of pain, consolation, and duty. However, at every step God is truly, physically present.

G. K. Chesterton speaks of Bethlehem this way: "It was here that a homeless couple had crept underground with the cattle when the doors of the crowded [inn][4] had been shut in their faces; and it was here beneath the very feet of the passersby, in a cellar under the very floor of the world, that Jesus Christ was born."[5] What an incredible statement! The Holy Family was a "homeless couple"! The Holy Family, who are home for all humanity, are homeless. Their home is so humble that it can fit all mankind within it, with room to spare, despite there being "no room at the inn" for them.

Venerable Fulton J. Sheen also describes this paradox of God being homeless in His own creation:

> If the artist is at home in his studio because the paintings are the creation of his own mind; if the sculptor is at home among his statues because they are the work of his own hands; if the husbandman is at home among his vines because he planted them; and if the father is at home among his children because they are his own, then surely, argues the world, he who made the world should be at home in it. He should come into it as an artist into his studio, and as a father into his home; but for the Creator to come among his creatures and be ignored by them; for God to come among his own and not be received by his own; for God to be homeless at home — that could only mean one thing to the worldly mind: the Babe could not have been God at all. And that is just why it missed him. *Divinity is always where one least expects to find it.*[6]

This paradox is why Christmas is a time for all humanity and all families to return home. The Holy Family, who makes a home for all of us, was without a home at Christmas. They are always guiding us home, but they were guided instead to the stable in the cave. "When all the scrolls and books of history are finally completed, counted, and measured down to the last line, the saddest line of all will be: 'There was no room in the inn.'"[7]

Christmas with Family

Why is it that the family comes together at Christmas? It's the call of moms and dads everywhere, especially our parents in Christ, to gather at Christmas. Saint Alphonsus Liguori said, "Arise, all ye nobles and peasants; Mary invites all, rich and poor, just and sinners, to enter the cave of Bethlehem, to adore and to kiss the feet of her new-born Son ... Let us enter; let us not be afraid."[8] It's through the Holy Family that all families are gathered together at Christmas. Mary and Joseph gather their family together at Christmas, just as once they gathered all their guests into the stable. Even though the cave and stable may seem like the last place you would want to entertain your Christmas guests, "now that [Jesus] is born and is lying on the straw, the cave is no longer horrible, but [has] become a paradise."[9] The Holy Family makes the inhospitable place into a beacon of hospitality for shepherds and kings alike and for us. They do this, however, not through rich adornments and decorations, but the warmth of their love. Saint Teresa of Calcutta offered this prayer for families at Christmas: "My prayer for you is that when Christ comes to you in Christmas, he may find in you a warm home, warm love like that of a heartful of love, like that of a simple shepherd who was the first one chosen to see Christ."[10]

Christmas spent with family may often seem like a time of contention and strife. Families can be so divided and broken. Nevertheless, despite all the odds against it, Christmas with family is often a place of healing, not hardship. This is true for individual families because it's true for the whole human family. This is true because of the first Christmas in Bethlehem:

> A helpless Newborn Child in a lowly cave restores dignity to every life being born, and brings hope to those overcome by doubt and discouragement. He has come to heal life's wounds and to restore meaning to death itself. In that Child, meek and defenseless, crying in a cold and bare cave, God has destroyed sin, and planted the seed of a new humanity, called to bring to fulfillment the original plan of creation and to transcend it through the grace of redemption.[11]
>
> — Pope St. John Paul II

The Heavenly Bread

> O Bread of Angels! Heavenly manna! Pearl of the Gospel! Sacrament of the present moment! Thou givest God under as lowly a form as the manger, the hay, or the straw. And to whom dost thou give him? "*Esurientes implevit bonis* — He has filled the hungry with good things" (Lk 1:53). God reveals himself to the humble under the most lowly forms, but the proud, attaching themselves entirely to that which is extrinsic, do not discover him hidden beneath, and are sent empty away.[12]
>
> — Fr. Jean-Pierre de Caussade

The name *Bethlehem* translates to "house of bread."[13] The "living bread which came down from heaven" (Jn 6:51) was laid in a *manger*, which means "a place to eat," a place for animals to eat. He who created the animals and the beasts now lays in their food trough. Here the beasts are accustomed to bow down. Here perhaps man, who lives like a beast, will also learn to bow down, taught by the Holy Family. He who created the sun to warm the cosmos is now being warmed by the breath of beasts. He who first breathed life into man takes His first breaths among beasts. His hands, which fashioned the stars, planets, and galaxies, are now bound in swaddling clothes and are too little to reach even the wet noses of the cattle and the donkey. In the dirtiest of all places is born purity Himself, who is able to cleanse all men with His Blood.

God appears in such a lowly form in the manger. In the same way, the Bread of Angels appears to us as ordinary bread. The Holy Family conceals the extraordinary beneath the ordinary, but this ordinariness is not merely a disguise or false facade. If God had to be born, the world would have expected for Him to be born in an inn at the very least. "The stable is a place for the outcasts, the ignored, the forgotten." According to Venerable Fulton Sheen, it "would be the last place in the world where one would have looked for him, [but again] *Divinity is always where one least expects to find it.*"[14]

The Holy Family also conceals the Heavenly Bread in order to protect it. The New Joseph protects the "bread … for the life of the world" (Jn 6:51), just as Joseph of Egypt stored up wheat for the years of famine and provided bread for the world:

> The seven years of plenty that prevailed in the land of Egypt came to an end; and the seven years of famine began to come, as Joseph had said. There was famine in all lands; but in all the land of Egypt there was bread. When all the land of Egypt was famished, the people cried to Pharaoh for bread; and Pharaoh said to all the Egyptians, *"Go to Joseph; and what he says to you, do."* So when the famine had spread over all the land, Joseph opened all the storehouses, and sold to the Egyptians, for the famine was severe in the land of Egypt. Moreover, all the earth came to Egypt to Joseph to buy grain, because the famine was severe over all the earth. (Gen 41:53–57, emphasis added)

Joseph of Egypt learned from Pharaoh's dreams that a famine was coming and that they needed to store up and protect the grain. Because he did this, Egypt was able to provide bread to the world. In the same way, St. Joseph learns from a dream that he must protect Jesus, the Bread of Life. Because St. Joseph did this, Jesus is able to provide bread to the world, His own flesh.

Just as Pharaoh entrusted Joseph with the royal treasuries and granaries, God entrusted St. Joseph with His greatest treasures, Mary and Jesus. Now, it's time that you entrust your treasures — your life, your hopes and dreams, and all your loved ones — to the protection of the Holy Family.

Pray the Litany of the Holy Family (page 207).

DAY 17

Holy Family, visited by the poor shepherds, have pity on us

And in that region there were shepherds out in the field, keeping watch over their flock by night. And an angel of the Lord appeared to them, and the glory of the Lord shone around them, and they were filled with fear. And the angel said to them, "Be not afraid; for behold, I bring you good news of a great joy which will come to all the people; for to you is born this day in the city of David a Savior, who is Christ the Lord. And this will be a sign for you: you will find a baby wrapped in swaddling cloths and lying in a manger." And suddenly there was with the angel a multitude of the heavenly host praising God and saying:

> "Glory to God in the highest, and on earth
> peace among men with whom he is pleased!"

When the angels went away from them into heaven, the shepherds said to one another, "Let us go over to Bethlehem and see this thing that has happened, which the Lord has made known to us." And they went with haste, and found Mary and Joseph, and the baby lying in a manger. And when they saw it they made known the saying which had been told them concerning this child; and all who heard it wondered at what the shepherds told them. But Mary kept all these things, pondering them in her heart. And the shepherds returned, glorifying and praising God for all they had heard and seen, as it had been told them.

— Lk 2:8–20

With that, St. Luke draws the curtain over the Christmas scene. Painters and poets, pastors and preachers have never seemed to exhaust this richest and most inimitable of scenes. Here, before the shepherds and the angels, the Holy Family makes its first appearance before men. Immediately, Joseph and Mary are the mediators through whom the shepherds come to Jesus. Through them, light spills down from angel-spangled Heaven, from the Star of Bethlehem, the new Glory Cloud. The light cascades through the Holy Family, whose mutual love is reflected in each of the faces of this earthly trinity. And then, the light bathes the shepherds and all visitors guided to the Holy Family, in the warm glow of the cold Bethlehem night.

Adoration is for everyone!

O come, all ye faithful, joyful and triumphant!
Adeste Fideles laeti triumphantes,
O come ye, O come ye, to Bethlehem.
Venite, venite in Bethlehem.
Come and behold him, born the King of angels;
Natum videte, Regem Angelorum;
O come, let us adore him, *Venite adoremus,*
O come, let us adore him, *Venite adoremus,*
O come, let us adore him, *Venite adoremus,*
Christ the Lord! *Dominum!*
See how the shepherds, summoned to his cradle,
En grege relicto, humiles ad cunas,
leaving their flocks, draw nigh to gaze.
vocati pastores approperant.
We too will thither bend our hearts' oblations;
Et nos ovanti gradu festinemus;
There shall we see him, his eternal Father's
Aeterni Parentis splendorem aeternum,
everlasting brightness now veiled under flesh.
velatum sub carne videbimus.

God shall we find there, a Babe in infant clothing;
Deum infantem, pannis involutum;
Child, for us sinners, poor, and in the manger,
Pro nobis egenum et foeno cubantem,
we would embrace thee, with love and awe.
piis foveamus amplexibus.
Who would not love thee, loving us so dearly?
Sic nos anamtem quis non redamaret?

In a certain sense, this famous Christmas carol is a hymn about adoration. Three times we cry out "*Venite adoremus!*" ("O come, let us adore him"). This song calls us home to adoration. It's fitting that the author of this hymn, John Francis Wade, was an English Catholic living in exile in France in the 18th century. The Anglican persecution of Catholics at this time in history, which went all the way back to Henry VIII and Elizabeth I, paralleled the persecution of the Jews during their exile. The Jews were living in exile, awaiting the birth of a Savior who would bring them home. In this hymn, the exile's desire to return home is palpable. But the hymn turns the desire for a return to our earthly home into a desire for our heavenly home; this desire is totally quenched simply by turning to the face of Jesus in adoration.

Read the words of the carol again, which call the shepherds and all the world to adoration: "*Adeste Fideles … Venite adoremus, Dominum!* O come, all ye faithful, O come, let us adore him, Christ the Lord!" Imagine the warmth of the light kissing the ruddy faces of the poor shepherds. It's the light of adoration. Adoration is for all of us — "all ye faithful." This is what the shepherds are teaching us. We are to seek the face of the Infant Jesus, just like they did. The shepherds resemble Mary as they approach Jesus. Like her, they went with "haste" (Lk 1:39; 2:16) after their annunciations by the angels. That's what this famous hymn, this Christmas carol, is calling us to do. This is how the hymn describes the shepherds: "See how the shepherds, summoned to his cradle, /

leaving their flocks, draw nigh to gaze. / We too will thither bend our hearts' oblations." Like the shepherds, Jesus calls to us to "draw nigh to gaze" at His face in the Eucharist. This is such a beautiful phrase for the way we are drawn to Jesus in adoration. Like He did for the shepherds, Jesus pulls us so close that the rest of the world and all its worries and cares are eclipsed by his "everlasting brightness now veiled." And like He did for the shepherds, Jesus draws us close to Himself through the Holy Family. Jesus draws us home through His own home.

The Poverty of God

> "Blessed are the poor in spirit, for theirs is the kingdom of heaven" (Mt 5:3).

God has a special love for the poor, so much so that He gives His entire kingdom over to the poor, as described in the Beatitude above. God also had a special love for the poor shepherds.

Think about all the major figures in salvation history who were shepherds. Shepherds, especially poor shepherds, filled a special role from the very beginning. Adam was a shepherd and steward over the entire animal kingdom. In this way, there's an archetypal connection between manhood and the shepherd. Shepherding is part of a man's very nature. Of Adam's sons, Cain was a farmer and Abel was a shepherd. God favored Abel's offering over Cain's, and Cain killed Abel out of jealousy. Noah was also a shepherd and steward over the entire animal kingdom, at least as many as he could fit on the Ark. Abraham, too, was a shepherd. He had whole caravans of sheep and other animals. Moses was also a shepherd. Importantly, Moses was "keeping the flock of his father-in-law, Jethro, the priest of Mid′ian" when he came to Mount Horeb and the Lord appeared to him as the burning bush (Ex 3:1–2).

And King David? David, a "man after God's own heart," whose name in Hebrew actually means "beloved" — what was his profession? When Goliath and the Philistines came to battle Israel, the boy David was tending "his father's sheep at Bethlehem" (1 Sam 17:15). King David wasn't just a shepherd; he was a shepherd in *Bethlehem*. It's no wonder that God sent His angels to announce the birth of His Son, first of all, to some of His favorite people, the poor shepherds of Bethlehem. But why would Jesus need to be born in such poverty? Why a stable instead of a palace?

Jesus is born in a stable so that He may abide in our hearts. Our souls are like stables. They're poor places, filled with squalor, and made filthy by our sin. Yet, the Divine Son sought us. He reached down into the depths of poverty, because that's where we are. And this, too, is the most startling lesson of the Holy Family: God's greatest riches appeared under the veil of poverty. This is the lesson of the Infant God of poverty. The greatest riches have nothing to do with wealth. Let the Holy Family help you reorder your understanding of poverty and riches.

Spiritual and Corporal Works of Mercy

Something mystical happens when we perform the Spiritual and Corporal Works of Mercy. One of the surest ways to learn the true nature of poverty, the hidden riches of poverty, is through performing them. By these Works of Mercy, we come to the aid of our neighbor in his spiritual and bodily poverty (see also Is 58:6–7; Heb 13:3). Jesus tells us in the Parable of the Sheep and the Goats (Mt 25:31–46) that we are truly serving Him when we serve people in poverty: "Truly, I say to you, as you did it to one of the least of these my brethren, you did it to me" (Mt 25:40). Jesus is not just speaking symbolically here. Do you want to see the face of Christ? Do the works of mercy.

As described in the Parable of the Sheep and the Goats, these are the seven Corporal Works of Mercy:

Feed the hungry
Give drink to the thirsty
Clothe the naked
Shelter the homeless
Visit the prisoners
Comfort the sick
Bury the dead

These are the seven Spiritual Works of Mercy (see also 1 Thess 5:11–18; Col 3:12–16):

Teach the ignorant
Pray for the living and the dead
Correct sinners
Counsel those in doubt
Console the sorrowful
Bear wrongs patiently
Forgive wrongs willingly

Not only are these works of mercy a mystical experience; they are also a great paradox. When we encounter people in their poverty, we encounter Jesus, who bestows on us all the riches of the universe. But poverty certainly doesn't look like riches. Poverty is smelly and repulsive. For many, the natural response to seeing people in poverty is to run away and ignore them. Poverty can also be rude and obnoxious. This is our typical response to people in spiritual poverty. Just as physical poverty can be repulsive to our physical senses, spiritual poverty can be repulsive to our spiritual senses. This can be a far greater form of revulsion. This is what makes practicing the Spiritual Works of Mercy more difficult, if not far more difficult, than the Corporal Works of Mercy. Who is in need of the Spiritual Works of Mercy? "The ignorant" are bigots and the hateful. "The doubtful" are atheists and cynics. "Sinners" embrace works of evil instead of works of mercy. All of these people inflict great wrongs on us, and we want to strike back. And yet, we are called to respond in exactly the opposite way.

Oftentimes, the greatest barrier to the Spiritual Works of Mercy is our own pride. Jesus calls to us from the other side of pride. And again, this is where we encounter Him and the great riches He offers us. Jesus also doesn't fail to reward us for overcoming our revulsion. For when we heal the sick or ransom the captives, or convert the ignorant or doubtful, we experience His own joy at finding the lost sheep and reuniting a lost soul with His Mystical Body. There's no greater joy than being the instrument of love through which a lost soul finds Jesus.

Consider how Our Lady and St. Joseph performed these Works of Mercy. By doing these works, we see Jesus face-to-face. Mary and Joseph beheld Jesus *face-to-face* every day. They tended to the Infant Jesus in His hunger, thirst, and nakedness. Every time Our Lady nursed Jesus, every time St. Joseph changed His swaddling clothes, they were performing works of mercy directly for Jesus Himself. When you do the Corporal Works of Mercy, do them in imitation of the Holy Family.

Imagine you are tending to the Infant Jesus. Or, if you are tending to the sick or dying, imagine you are easing the sufferings of Jesus on the Cross. You are. Now, think about all those whom the Holy Family encountered who were in need of spiritual mercy — all the ignorant who rejected Jesus, all the doubtful who left Him in disbelief, all the sinners who hated Him.

Think about how the Virgin Mary and St. Joseph bore these wrongs patiently. The Virgin Mary felt these wrongs so deeply that the same sword which pierced Jesus' Heart also "[pierced] through her own soul" (Lk 2:35). Think about how the Blessed Mother comforted the afflicted Christ on the Cross.

And lastly, think about how both Mary and Joseph are unceasingly praying for the living and the dead even now. When you enter into these repulsive places to perform works of mercy, know that you are truly entering the Holy House of Nazareth. There, alongside the Holy Family, you'll experience unfathomable intimacy with Jesus.

Pray the Litany of the Holy Family (page 207).

DAY 18

Holy Family, obliged to live in a stable, have pity on us

> The old trinity was of father and mother and child and is called the human family. The new is of child and mother and father and has the name of the Holy Family. It is in no way altered except in being entirely reversed; just as the world which is transformed was not in the least different, except in being turned upside down ... This sketch of the human story began in a cave; the cave which popular science associates with the caveman and in which practical discovery has really found archaic drawings of animals. The second half of human history, which was like a new creation of the world, also begins in a cave ... A mass of legend and literature, which increases and will never end, has repeated and rung the changes on that single paradox; that the hands that had made the sun and stars were too small to reach the huge heads of the cattle ... There is in this buried divinity an idea of undermining the world; of shaking the towers and palaces from below; even as Herod the great king felt that earthquake under him and swayed with his swaying palace.[1]
>
> — G. K. Chesterton

Chesterton writes thus of the paradox of the cave or the stable. Caves were often used as natural shelters, or stables, for animals in Bethlehem and across Israel at the time of Christ's birth. What occurred in that tiny cave in Bethlehem is simultaneously fulfilling the past while presaging the future, cosmic in significance yet very intimate, peaceful but earth-shattering. Jesus is the New Adam, the new firstborn of creation. It's fitting, then, that this newborn-ancient Child should be found in a cave.

It's also fitting that He who would "undermine" all the civilizations and empires of the world should be born underground, because He's the hidden epicenter of the coming "earthquake" that will reshape the entire world. Jesus is born at the bottom of civilization, both physically in the cave and socio-economically in the stable, but His hour is coming when He will turn the world upside down. Jesus was born in the earth and will one day descend to the abode of the dead to free the souls waiting there. He will also one day ascend to the throne of the King of Kings in Heaven.

Seek First the Kingdom of God!

Delivering a baby on the road would be a very stressful experience. Many children have been born on the roadside *en route* to the hospital, but the backseat of a car is still preferable to the stable. God was teaching the Holy Family to rely on Him alone. It's fitting that the Child born in this cave would one day tell us the following:

> Therefore I tell you, do not be anxious about your life, what you shall eat or what you shall drink, nor about your body, what you shall put on. Is not life more than food, and the body more than clothing? Look at the birds of the air: they neither sow nor reap nor gather into barns, and yet your heavenly Father feeds them. Are you not of more value than they? ... Therefore do not be anxious, saying, "What shall we eat?" or "What shall we drink?" or "What shall we wear?" For the Gentiles seek all these things; and your heavenly Father knows that you need them all. But seek first his kingdom and his righteousness, and all these things shall be yours as well. (Mt 6:25–26, 31–33)

What better example do we have of seeking first the Kingdom of God than the Holy Family? Being obliged to live in a stable was among the least of their sacrifices. All three members of the Holy Family were given multiple opportunities to offer up their lives. They never hesitated. More than that, Mary and Joseph were the parents of the "Lamb of God," born, as lambs are, in the stable. The meaning of this was always before them. Myrrh was given to the Baby Jesus to prophesy that His sacrificial Body would one day be anointed with it in death. Mary and Joseph, like Sarah and Abraham before them, were always prepared to give all things to God, even their Son, who was God Himself. Such perfect faith!

We have here no lasting city

Just as Jesus was born outside the walls of Bethlehem, He would one day be crucified outside the walls of Jerusalem. This all points to the city which is to come, our future home:

> So Jesus also suffered outside the gate in order to sanctify the people through his own blood. Therefore let us go forth to him outside the camp, bearing abuse for him. For we have here no lasting city, but we seek the city which is to come. Through him then let us continually offer up a sacrifice of praise to God, that is, the fruit of lips that acknowledge his name. Do not neglect to do good and to share what you have, for such sacrifices are pleasing to God. (Heb 13:12–16)

Wherever the Holy Family is, that's our home. Everything else is just temporary. It doesn't last. As St. Thérèse of Lisieux said, "The world is thy ship, not thy home."[2] We look instead to the *ever*-lasting city. Everything we do in this life is an opportunity for greater union with Jesus. Behind every temptation is hidden another step towards Jesus. All of our joys and sufferings ultimately point to our destiny in Heaven, our eternal home with Jesus. Who knew this better than the Holy Family? Both their earthly and eternal home were and are with Jesus. The Holy Family had on earth what we will find in Heaven. Their ordinary life will be our eternal life. They experienced in life what we will experience in eternity. This is why we unite ourselves to the Holy Family: union with the Holy Family unites our life on earth with life in Heaven. The home of Nazareth is a foretaste of our home in Heaven.

Love finds a way

Perhaps we haven't spoken enough of the love that abides in the Holy Family. We have spoken of their function in history, theology, and our salvation, but we haven't begun to plumb the depths of the great love that existed between the members of the Holy Family. One important question that helps us understand the nature of this love is this: What is the function of this love? What is the power of this love?

When it comes to the Holy Family and the Christ Child, all the rules seem to fade away. Natural laws and restrictions like natural conception or even natural childbirth seem not to apply. The economic and social rules for poverty — that poverty is a place of sadness and despair, and certainly no place for kings and queens — just don't apply either. Rules of power and dominance don't seem to affect the Holy Family, as God "[puts] down the mighty from their thrones and [exalts] those of low degree" (Lk 1:52). Even the so-called ultimate power of the kings of the world to determine life and death can't stop Jesus, who, by His death, conquers the world.

All the rules seem to fall away before the Holy Family. Love finds a way to triumph by surmounting the rules of the world, rules manipulated by Satan to control and malign. But this isn't true, not exactly. The Holy Family reveals the true rules. They reveal them to us and to a world that has never really understood these rules. Even as we admire the Holy Family, we are often still stuck in a misconception of the world wrought by the devil. The devil contorts the true rules, the law of God, to achieve power, dominance, and ultimately death. The true rules declare that sacrificial love always wins, always conquers. They also proclaim that humility is more powerful than might and that the real power over life and death is not wielded by tyrants, but by God, the Lord of Life and Resurrection. The Holy Family follows the true rules and truly conquers the world. The Holy Family is not the exception; they are the rule. They are not defenseless before King Herod; King Herod is powerless before them. Love always finds a way, because love is the fundamental law. Love is the deeper law, the original law, that supersedes all of Satan's power and lies. Satan's main goal is to distract us from this very simple truth, but the Holy Family, obliged to live in the stable, is too powerful an icon of truth and beauty to be overlooked. The Holy Family unravels all of Satan's lies.

Pray the Litany of the Holy Family (page 207).

DAY 19

Holy Family, praised by the angels, have pity on us

> And [the angel Gabriel] came to her and said, "Hail, full of grace, the Lord is with you!" ... And the angel said to her, "Do not be afraid, Mary, for you have found favor with God. And behold, you will conceive in your womb and bear a son, and you shall call his name Jesus."
>
> — Lk 1:28, 30

> Behold, an angel of the Lord appeared to him in a dream, saying, "Joseph, son of David, do not fear to take Mary your wife, for that which is conceived in her is of the Holy Spirit; she will bear a son, and you shall call his name Jesus, for he will save his people from their sins."
>
> — Mt 1:20–21

> Then the devil left [Jesus], and behold, angels came and ministered to him.
>
> — Mt 4:11

The angels are constantly praising, pointing to, and ministering to the Holy Family. Look how Mary is greeted by the Archangel Gabriel. This is no ordinary greeting. The archangel "hails" Mary. The Gospels reserve this greeting for Mary and Jesus alone: "Hail, Full of Grace" and "Hail, King of the Jews."[1] In both of these royal greetings, their names are omitted. Instead, their royal titles are used. Jesus' royal title is "King of the Jews," and Mary's royal title is "Full of Grace."[2] More than just her royal title, it is her *heavenly* title, for it is supplied by no less a personage than the Archangel Gabriel, Heaven's own messenger, who is empowered to announce God's will to mankind. This is high praise indeed.

The clouds of Heaven so surrounded the Holy Family that the angels were their constant companions. The angels appeared to guide every thought and step of Mary and Joseph, to resolve their least confusion and their greatest fears. The angels were the constant ministers and house guests of the Holy Family. "Yes, I want to be in that number," the old song goes, "when the saints go marching in." But why wait? Be a member of that same holy household now. Abide now in that small home of saints and angels, which was humble enough to contain all the clouds of Heaven.

The Choirs of Angels

> God loves in the Seraphim, as charity,
> knows in the Cherubim, as truth,
> is seated in the Thrones, as equity,
> reigns in the Dominions, as majesty,
> rules in the Principalities, as principle,
> guards in the Powers, as salvation,
> acts in the Virtues, as strength,
> reveals in the Archangels, as light,
> assists in the Angels, as piety.[3]
>
> — St. Bernard of Clairvaux

"And suddenly there was with the angel a multitude of the heavenly host praising God and saying, 'Glory to God in the highest, and on earth peace among men with whom he is pleased!'" (Lk 2:13–14). Can you imagine the Choirs of Angels arranged above the place of Jesus' birth? The skies overhead are full of the light of these multitudes, while below the world slumbers. Since the creation of the universe, has such a momentous event ever passed so unnoticed? God uses His angels to direct mankind to what is truly important, and the angels are pointing to the Holy Family.

Nine "Choirs" or types of angels are identified in the Bible. These classifications have been elaborated upon by various theologians, such as St. Thomas Aquinas, according to the following schema:[4]

The first three Choirs see and adore God directly. They are (1) Seraphim, (2) Cherubim, and (3) Thrones. *Seraphim* means "the burning ones," so named because of their proximity to God and their most intense "flaming" love for God. The seraphim comprehend God with the greatest clarity. Lucifer is traditionally identified as a fallen seraphim whose beautiful light was changed into darkness.[5] *Cherubim*, which means "fullness of wisdom," contemplate God's Divine Providence and plan for His creatures. Lastly, the *Thrones* symbolize Divine Justice and judicial power and contemplate God's power and justice. As we go through the nine Choirs, think about how, rank on rank, all these Choirs are pointing to the Holy Family. The Cherubim point to the Holy Family as the heart of God's Divine Providence and plan for humanity. In the Old Testament, the wings of the two carved golden Cherubim stretched out across the top of the Ark of the Covenant (Ex 25:20); now again in the New Testament we find their wings sheltering the New Ark, Mary, and the entire Holy Family. The Cherubim of Genesis blocked the first family from returning to the Tree of Life (Gen 3:24); now the Cherubim point the way to the Holy Family, which is the New Tree of Life and its fruit. The Thrones point to the Holy Family as the seat of God's power and justice. Each rank imbues the Holy Family with its own gifts.

The next three Choirs fulfill God's providential plan for the universe; in this plan the Holy Family, and the family in general, is the critical element. The second sphere of Choirs includes (4) the *Dominions*, whose name evokes authority and who govern the lesser Choirs of Angels; (5) the *Virtues*, who implement the orders from the Dominions and govern the heavenly bodies between Heaven and earth; and (6) the *Powers*, who confront and fight against any evil forces opposed to God's providential plan.[6] We think about how these forces of angels were arrayed around the Holy Family to protect God's plan of salvation, and how consecration to the Holy Family connects us to this great order who protects from evil and disorder.

The last three Choirs are directly involved in human affairs. These are (7) the *Principalities*, who care for earthly principalities, such as nations or cities; (8) the *Archangels*, who deliver God's most important messages to mankind; and (9) the *Angels*, properly speaking, who serve as our "guardian angels" and ministers. Now, consider St. Paul's words that Christ is "far above all rule and authority and power and dominion and above every name that is named, not only in this age but also in that which is to come; and [the Father] has put all things under his feet" (Eph 1:21–22). Those same feet, which would one day be pierced on Calvary, lay still and swaddled beneath all the Choirs of Angels in Bethlehem. At the center of all human affairs is placed the Holy Family. This last sphere of angels ministers to the Holy Family so that its order may ripple out as the fundamental plan for all human affairs.

Your Guardian Angel

> Do you not greet warmly all the people you love, and speak to them cordially? — Well, you and I are going to greet Jesus, Mary and Joseph, and our Guardian Angels, many times a day.[7]
>
> — St. Josemaría Escrivá

Do you want to live in the humble home of Nazareth? Then prepare yourself for an angel-packed home life. The angels seem to have been always swirling around the Holy Family. The air must have been thick with them, like another Glory Cloud composed entirely of angels.

One of the most wondrous and practical aspects of consecration to Mary, according to St. Louis de Monfort, is the supreme good it does for us at the Particular Judgment.

The Particular Judgment is the individual judgment of each of us by God, which occurs immediately after death. This is when the eternal destiny of each soul, newly separated from the body, is decided by the undeniable and just judgment of God. We pray that Mary is our Advocate at this most critical moment in a special way provided through consecration. This most critical moment of our lives, the Particular Judgment, also involves the most important aspects of the Marian consecration. The key request and feature of this Marian spirituality is summarized by St. Louis de Montfort's "Prayer to Mary":

> May your virtues take the place of my sins; may your merits be my only adornment in the sight of God and make up for all that is wanting in me. Finally, dearly beloved Mother, grant, if it be possible, that I may have no other spirit but yours to know Jesus and His divine will; that I may have no other soul but yours to praise and glorify the Lord; that I may have no other heart but yours to love God with a love as pure and ardent as yours.[8]

The supreme gift, therefore, of Marian consecration is that when we stand before God at our Particular Judgment, we will be adorned with Mary's virtues and merits, not our own.[9]

It's all the more interesting then that our guardian angels are the ones tasked with recording all our good works. According to St. John Vianney, "The devil writes down our sins — our guardian angel all our merits. Labor that the guardian angel's book may be full, and the devil's empty."[10] Our guardian angels always accompany us as the principal witnesses of our actions, and at our judgment they will be the principal witnesses for *the* defense, our defense. At our Particular Judgment, they will remember the kind deeds we performed for our Lord throughout our lives. Our guardian angel comforts us with these merits, too. "When you feel lost before the terrible accusations of the enemy, your Angel will present those intimate desires of your heart — which perhaps you yourself might have forgotten — those proofs of love which you might have had for God the Father, God the Son, [and] God the Holy Spirit."[11] That is why you must never forget your guardian angel, the Prince of Heaven assigned to you who will not abandon you, now or at that decisive moment of judgment.

Now imagine yourself asking your guardian angel for your book of merits and place it at the feet of the Holy Family. Tuck it in between the bits of straw beneath Jesus' manger. It's a most special gift and sacrifice, a special kind of poverty, to give all our merits to the Holy Family and risk standing naked before God's judgment seat. But Mary and Joseph won't be outdone in generosity. In exchange for our merits, they will adorn us with their own endless virtues and merits. They will take us as their own naked child, enfold us in the swaddling clothes of their own merits — as once they wrapped their own Son — and present us to Him whom they once cared for; and thus adorned will we be on our judgment day.

St. Michael the Archangel

> Whenever a mighty deed is in question, Michael is assigned, so that by his actions and name, which means "Who is like God?," it may be made known that no one can do what God can do.[12]
>
> — Pope St. Gregory the Great

In Revelation 12, the dragon, "that ancient serpent, who is called the Devil and Satan" (Rev 12:9) is shown in three places. In the first place, the dragon is standing before the Virgin Mary as she is about to bear the Christ Child that he "might devour her child when she brought it forth" (Rev 12:4). In the second place, the dragon is standing before "Michael and his angels fighting against [him]" (Rev 12:7).

In the third place, after the dragon "saw that he had been thrown down to the earth, he pursued the woman who had borne the male child," but the woman is "given the two wings of the great eagle that she might fly from the serpent into the wilderness" (Rev 12:13–14).

Christ is not the only child "brought forth" from the Blessed Mother and attacked by the dragon in all these accounts. The new birth of Baptism, through which we all become Christ's brothers and sisters, occurs in the spiritual womb of the New Eve and mother of all the living, the Blessed Mother. So our births, too, are being attacked by the dragon. In all of this, the Holy Family is not alone. Revelation describes St. Michael as the Holy Family's constant companion throughout all these travails. Saint Michael the Archangel is always standing guard beside the Holy Family. When we consecrate ourselves to the Holy Family, we place ourselves in the shelter of the wings of God's mightiest angel as well. Satan recoils in fright from even our guardian angels. Can you imagine, then, how safe we are standing beside St. Michael?

Let's conclude this section by invoking the aid of St. Michael the Archangel. You're probably familiar with the shortened version of the "Prayer to St. Michael." Here is the longer version of this prayer, as it was originally composed by Pope Leo XIII in 1898 after he experienced a dramatic vision during Holy Mass:

> O Glorious Archangel St. Michael, Prince of the heavenly host, be our defense in the terrible warfare which we carry on against principalities and powers, against the rulers of this world of darkness, and spirits of evil.
>
> Come to the aid of man, whom God created immortal, made in his own image and likeness, and redeemed at a great price from the tyranny

of the devil. Fight this day the battle of the Lord, together with the holy angels, as already thou hast fought the leader of the proud angels, Lucifer, and his apostate host, who were powerless to resist thee, nor was there place for them any longer in heaven. That cruel, that ancient serpent, who is called the devil or Satan, who seduces the whole world, was cast into the abyss with his angels.

Behold, this primeval enemy and slayer of men has taken courage. Transformed into an angel of light, he wanders about with all the multitude of wicked spirits, invading the earth in order to blot out the name of God and of his Christ, to seize upon, slay and cast into eternal perdition souls destined for the crown of eternal glory. This wicked dragon pours out, as a most impure flood, the venom of his malice on men, his depraved mind, corrupt heart, his spirit of lying, impiety, blasphemy, his pestilential breath of impurity and of every vice and iniquity. These most crafty enemies have filled and inebriated with gall and bitterness the Church, the Spouse of the Immaculate Lamb, and have laid impious hands on her most sacred possessions. In the Holy Place itself, where has been set up the See of the most holy Peter and the Chair of Truth for the light of the world, they have raised the throne of their abominable impiety, with the iniquitous design that when the Pastor has been struck, the sheep may be scattered.

Arise then, O invincible Prince, bring help against the attacks of the lost spirits to the people of God, and give them the victory. They venerate thee as their protector and patron; in thee Holy Church glories as her defense against the malicious power of hell; to thee has God entrusted the souls of men to be established in heavenly beatitude. Oh, pray to the God of peace that he may put Satan under our feet, so far conquered that he may no longer be able to hold men in captivity and harm the Church. Offer our prayers in the sight of the Most High, so that they may quickly conciliate the mercies of the Lord; and beating down the dragon, the ancient serpent who is the devil and Satan, do thou again make him captive in the abyss, that he may no longer seduce the nations. Amen.

Behold the Cross of the Lord;
be scattered, hostile powers.
The Lion of the tribe of Judah has conquered,
the root of David.
Let thy mercies be upon us, O Lord,
As we have hoped in thee.
O Lord, hear my prayer.
And let my cry come unto thee.

Let us pray:

God, the Father of our Lord Jesus Christ, we call upon thy holy name, and we humbly implore thy clemency, that by the intercession of Mary, ever Virgin Immaculate and our Mother, and of the glorious Archangel St. Michael, thou wouldst deign to help us against Satan and all other unclean spirits, who wander about the world for the injury of the human race and the ruin of souls. Amen.

Pray the Litany of the Holy Family (page 207).

DAY 20

Holy Family, venerated by the Wise Men from the East, have pity on us

We return again to the Glory Cloud (in Hebrew *shekinah*), the great pillar of cloud and fire that accompanied Moses and the people of Israel through all their wanderings in the wilderness:

> And the Lord went before them by day in a pillar of cloud to lead them along the way, and by night in a pillar of fire to give them light, that they might travel by day and by night; the pillar of cloud by day and the pillar of fire by night did not depart from before the people. (Ex 13:21–22)

> Therefore thou didst provide a flaming pillar of fire as a guide for thy people's unknown journey, and a harmless sun for their glorious wandering. For their enemies deserved to be deprived of light and imprisoned in darkness, those who had kept thy sons imprisoned, through whom the imperishable light of the law was to be given to the world. (Wis 18:3–4)

> In that day the branch of the Lord shall be beautiful and glorious, and the fruit of the land shall be the pride and glory of the survivors of Israel. And he who is left in Zion and remains in Jerusalem will be called holy, every one who has been recorded for life in Jerusalem, when the Lord shall have washed away the filth of the daughters of Zion and cleansed the bloodstains of Jerusalem from its midst by a spirit of judgment and by a spirit of burning. Then the Lord will create over the whole site of Mount Zion and over her assemblies a cloud by day, and smoke and the shining of a flaming fire by night;

> for over all the glory there will be a canopy and a pavilion. It will be for a shade by day from the heat, and for a refuge and a shelter from the storm and rain. (Is 4:2–6)

Now the time prophesied by Isaiah has come for Israel. Jesus, the "righteous branch" of the Lord, has been born to us. He is "beautiful and glorious." He has been born from the broken family tree of King David, the stump of Jesse. The filth and bloodstains will be washed away by Jesus' Blood, and the remnant of survivors in Jerusalem will be made holy, beginning with the Holy Family. Over all this, there will be a great cloud by day and a flaming fire by night. This is the return of the Glory Cloud, the pillar of fire and smoke. The Glory Cloud rises over the Holy Family in Bethlehem. The Glory Cloud is their stable, their refuge and shelter from the storm and rain. It's the great light of Bethlehem rising over the Holy Family, the imperishable light given for the world. The Glory Cloud has returned as the Star of Bethlehem. It's the light to the nations that brings the three kings of the foreign nations, the Wise Men, to Jesus.

There's only one way to Heaven: Jesus

> When they had heard the king they went their way; and lo, the star which they had seen in the East went before them, till it came to rest over the place where the child was. When they saw the star, they rejoiced exceedingly with great joy; and going into the house they saw the child with Mary his mother, and they fell down and worshiped him. Then, opening their treasures, they offered him gifts, gold and frankincense and myrrh. And being warned in a dream not to return to Herod, they departed to their own country by another way.
>
> — Mt 2:9–12

God is being so direct, so simple. The Star of Bethlehem, the return of the Glory Cloud to Israel, is a giant beam of light from Heaven to Jesus. It guides the shepherds and the wise men alike to Jesus and the Holy Family. The purpose is to direct them through Jesus to Heaven.

God's message to the Three Wise Men from the East is simple: Go to My Son, go to Heaven. The heavens are directing you to My Son; My Son will lead you to Heaven. The Three Wise Men represent the ancient eastern religions.[1] God reached out to all these through the great sign of the Star of Bethlehem. His statement to the Wise Men is clear: Go to Jesus.

The Wise Men's response to Jesus is also clear and fitting. They adored and venerated Him. The Gospel says that the Wise Men "fell down and worshiped him" (Mt 2:11). They were converted and emptied themselves of their former treasures: gold and frankincense and myrrh. They no longer treasured their former religions, for they had found a new, far greater, treasure in Christ. Then, finally, they returned to their countries as different men, for they "departed to their own country *by another way*" (Mt 2:12, emphasis added). The way they had come to Jesus, through "the ancient superstitions of the Gentiles,"[2] was not the way they returned home from adoring Jesus.

Bring the Nations to Jesus!

> When they reached Bethlehem, the Magi adored the divine Child and offered him symbolic gifts, becoming forerunners of the peoples and nations which down the centuries never cease to seek and meet Christ.[3]
>
> —Pope St. John Paul II

The Magi represented all the nations in their search for a heavenly King. Their actions of adoring Jesus and offering

Him royal gifts demonstrated that they did indeed find this new heavenly kind of King. "[C]ontent with testimony of the star alone, they adored: for they saw a man, and they acknowledged God."[4] The Magi demonstrated the future faith of the nations, because the King they found surpassed all human understanding. Though the stable showed no indication of earthly royal power whatsoever, it was on full display in the heavens. The Magi "gaze in deep wonder at what they see: Heaven on earth, earth in Heaven, man in God, God in man, one whom the whole universe cannot contain now enclosed in a tiny body."[5]

The Magi were just the beginning of an endless parade of nations, who each in turn come to acknowledge and glorify the Holy Family. Isaiah prophesied all this: "[N]ations shall come to your light, and kings to the brightness of your rising. … the wealth of the nations shall come to you. … They shall bring gold and frankincense, … and I will glorify my glorious house." (Is 60:3, 5–7). God will glorify His "glorious house," the Holy Family, by expanding it to include all nations through Baptism. In this, the Magi prefigure the Great Commission: "Go therefore and make disciples of all nations, baptizing them in the name of the Father and of the Son and of the Holy Spirit" (Mt 28:19). Through this Baptism, all nations will be adopted into the family of God. Through the Holy Trinity and the Holy Family, the earthly trinity, it's possible for all nations to come to the heavenly Trinity.

Bring the Nations to Catholicism!

> The men of whom Matthew speaks were not just astronomers. They were "wise." They represent the inner dynamic of religion towards self-transcendence, which involves a search for truth, a search for the true God and hence "philosophy" in the original sense of the word. Wisdom, then, serves to purify the message of "science": the rationality

> of that message does not remain at the level of the intellectual knowledge, but seeks understanding in its fullness, and so raises reason to its loftiest possibilities.[6]
>
> — Pope Benedict XVI

Like all the nations that stream to Jesus, all systems of thought are brought to fullness in Catholicism. All schools of philosophy, all fields of science, and all other religions see only partially, as "as in a mirror, dimly" (1 Cor 13:12). But in the stable, under the watchful gaze of the Holy Family, the Wise Men see Truth "face to face." The Wise Men represent the quest of the wise and learned for ultimate Truth. Their quest ends in a very unlikely place. Ultimate Truth is not to be found in the great halls of learning or the marble palaces of kings but in the stable, in the arms of Mary and Joseph. By the light of the star, Heaven is directing the wise to the Holy Family, to a Babe in a manger. Here is the Catholic Church in its infancy.

The Magi represent the movement of men devoted to worldly wisdom from out of the depths of error to the true light of Catholicism. "Whatever new light illumines the darkness of their hearts," says Pope St. Leo the Great, "comes from the rays of the same star."[7] The threefold gifts of the Wise Men are "repeated in the hearts of true believers" and offered to Jesus by all who embrace the One, Holy, Catholic, and Apostolic Faith.[8] The true believer who "acknowledges Christ the King of the universe brings gold from the treasure of his heart; he that believes the Only-begotten of God to have united man's true nature to himself, offers myrrh; and he that confesses him in no wise inferior to the Father's majesty, worships him in a manner with incense."[9]

These same treasures of the Magi flow into the heart of every Catholic who places himself before the Holy Family. As described above, these are the reign, the doctrine, and the liturgy of the Church. In the Church, one enjoys the reign of the King of the universe, the sound doctrine of beliefs, and the correct manner of worship in the Divine Liturgy. We consecrate ourselves to the Holy Family so that the darkness of our hearts will be illuminated by the rays of the same star and overflow with the treasures of Catholicism.

Pray the Litany of the Holy Family (page 207).

DAY 21

Holy Family, greeted by the pious Simeon in the Temple, have pity on us

> And when the time came for their purification according to the law of Moses, they brought [Jesus] up to Jerusalem to present him to the Lord (as it is written in the law of the Lord, "Every male that opens the womb shall be called holy to the Lord") and to offer a sacrifice according to what is said in the law of the Lord, "a pair of turtledoves, or two young pigeons." Now there was a man in Jerusalem, whose name was Simeon, and this man was righteous and devout, looking for the consolation of Israel, and the Holy Spirit was upon him. And it had been revealed to him by the Holy Spirit that he should not see death before he had seen the Lord's Christ.
>
> — Lk 2:22–26

After the birth of Jesus, the Holy Family went to the Temple in Jerusalem "for their purification," meaning the purification of Jesus and Mary. It's jarring to think of Jesus and Mary, who have no need to be purified, being required to undergo a "purification." Nevertheless, this purification is required by the Law of Moses (see Lev 12:1–8). Jesus will later say, "Think not that I have come to abolish the law and the prophets; I have come not to abolish them but to fulfill them" (Mt 5:17). This is a strong statement, and Jesus strengthens it even further, saying that "till heaven and earth pass away, not an iota, not a dot, will pass from the law until all is accomplished" (Mt 5:18). The iotas and dots were the smallest of marks in the Hebrew alphabet, not even words, much less laws. This is why we see the two purest souls since the dawn of Creation presenting themselves for purification.

On top of this, poverty is added to this jarring situation. This is the family of the Lamb of God, who takes away the sins of the world — but this family can't afford to buy a lamb. There is no lamb of purification offered for the Lamb of God, who will give His Blood to purify the entire world. Instead, the Holy Family can only afford to offer two turtledoves. Despite all the twists of irony, there is something fitting in the Holy Family offering doves, the symbol for the Holy Spirit. One dove is for Mary, the spouse of the Holy Spirit; and one dove is for Jesus, who was conceived by the Holy Spirit, with whom Jesus is co-equal. Further, the Holy Family comes upon Simeon, about whom it is said that "the Holy Spirit was upon him" (Lk 2:25). And, it had been revealed to Simeon "by the Holy Spirit that he should not see death before he had seen the Lord's Christ" (Lk 2:26).

This is not to say that the Presentation of the Holy Family is without effect or importance. The Holy Spirit, in the form of the Glory Cloud (*shekinah*), had left the Temple shortly before its destruction by the Babylonians in 586 B.C. (see Ezek 10:18–19). Now, the Holy Spirit returns. Also, when Mary and Joseph give Jesus to the priest to be offered to God, they're uniting themselves in that offering. They're giving everything they are and everything they have. In short, the Holy Family was formally consecrating itself to God. The closeness of this union excelled any previous covenant, because the Holy Family also contained God Himself. In consecrating ourselves to the Holy Family, we, too, are invited into this closest of unions.

The Suffering Savior

> And inspired by the Spirit [Simeon] came into the temple; and when the parents brought in the child Jesus, to do for him according to the custom of the law, he took him up in his arms and blessed God and said, "Lord, now lettest thou thy servant depart in peace, according to thy word; for mine eyes have seen thy salvation which thou hast prepared in the

> presence of all peoples, a light for revelation to the Gentiles, and for glory to thy people Israel.
>
> — Lk 2:27–32

On that day 2,000 years ago at the Temple in Jerusalem, Joseph and Mary were the first to hear those sweet, somber, hopeful words from Simeon's lips: "Lord, now lettest thou thy servant depart in peace," which is called the *Nunc Dimittis.* At the end of every day, these are the last words prayed by the Universal Church in the Liturgy of the Hours, and this has been the case for most of Church history.[1] How many nameless saints have gone on to their reward with Simeon's words among their last?

What is this great hope which is fulfilled in Simeon's presence? As had been revealed to him by the Holy Spirit, Simeon "should not see death before he had seen the Lord's Christ," the Savior of Israel, the Messiah.

The Sorrowful Mother

> And his father and his mother marveled at what was said about him; and Simeon blessed them and said to Mary his mother, "Behold, this child is set for the fall and rising of many in Israel, and for a sign that is spoken against (and a sword will pierce through your own soul also), that thoughts out of many hearts may be revealed."
>
> — Lk 2:33–35

Just as the gift of myrrh pointed to the death of Jesus, the words of Simeon again point to the future suffering of the Holy Family. Jesus' death was always before them. Inspired by the Holy Spirit, Simeon prophesied Our Lady's role as the Mother of Sorrows and Queen of Martyrs. Regarding Mary's role during the Crucifixion, the Lenten hymn "*Stabat Mater*" eloquently describes Mary standing beside the Cross as the Mother of Sorrows. Here is a selection of stanzas from this ancient hymn:

> At the cross her station keeping,
> Stood the mournful Mother weeping,
> Close to Jesus to the last.
>
> Through her heart, his sorrow sharing,
> All his bitter anguish bearing,
> Now at length the sword had passed. …
>
> Christ above in torment hangs.
> She beneath beholds the pangs
> Of her dying glorious Son. …
>
> Bruised, derided, cursed, defiled,
> She beheld her tender Child,
> All with bloody scourges rent. …
>
> O thou Mother: fount of love!
> Touch my spirit from above,
> Make my heart with thine accord.
>
> Make me feel as thou hast felt;
> Make my soul to glow and melt
> With the love of Christ, my Lord.
>
> Holy Mother, pierce me through,
> In my heart each wound renew
> Of my Savior crucified. …
>
> Christ, when thou shalt call me hence,
> Be thy Mother my defense,
> Be thy Cross my victory.[2]

Imagine seeing your beloved child undergoing such physical and emotional agony while you're utterly powerless to stop it. Many parents, all too many, don't have to imagine this. But now imagine that this child is dear, not just to you, but to the entire world. Every life in history depends on this one child.

Regarding the Blessed Mother's sorrow at the Cross, St. Bonaventure writes that "no grief was more bitter than hers, because no son was as dear as her Son."[3] He also remarks that "those wounds — which were scattered over the body of our Lord — were all united in the single heart of Mary."[4] Saint Lawrence Justinian expresses this same idea: "The heart of Mary became, as it were, a mirror of the Passion of the Son, in which might be seen, faithfully reflected, the spitting, the blows and wounds, and all that Jesus suffered."[5] Mary endured so much suffering at Christ's side that she is called the Queen of Martyrs. Saint Ildephonsus asserted that "to say that Mary's sorrows were greater than all the torments of the martyrs united, was to say too little."[6] Saint Anselm adds to this, saying that "the most cruel tortures inflicted on the holy martyrs were trifling, or as nothing in comparison with the martyrdom of Mary."[7]

Even though Mary's suffering at the Cross would take place over 30 years in the future, Simeon's prophecy reminded her of what was to come, as she "kept all these things, pondering them in her heart" (Lk 2:19). This haunting prophecy prepared Mary for this trial, which would test even the supreme heights of her sanctity and generosity — and not just Mary, but Joseph, too. Although he died before the Crucifixion of Jesus, he also suffered from the specter of the thought of his family being tortured in his absence.

The Consoling Joseph

Just as Mary is called the "Mother of Sorrows," Joseph can be called the "Father of Sorrows." As there is a traditional devotion to the "Seven Sorrows of Mary," there is also a devotion to the "Seven Sorrows of Joseph," the fourth of which is hearing Simeon's painful, prophetic message. Why then did Simeon not prophesy that a sword would pierce Joseph's soul as well? He would surely suffer the sword along with his wife and Son, *if* he were still alive. Indirectly, therefore, Simeon's prophecy tells us that Joseph is going to die before the hour of their suffering. Because of this, Joseph endures an entirely different kind of suffering.

Imagine how Joseph must have suffered as a husband and a father upon hearing that the hour was coming when his beloved wife and Son would suffer such savage torments. Even worse, the hour was approaching — and he would not be there to protect and comfort them. There's something in the nature of manhood that desires to act and do — "Be doers of the word, and not hearers only" (Jas 1:22). "'Repairer of the breach,' they shall call you, 'Restorer of ruined dwellings'" (Is 58:12, NABRE). Saint Joseph epitomizes manhood in his action. He is a carpenter, creating and repairing with his hands. At the word of the angel, in the dark of night, he immediately moves his family to Egypt. And yet, he can do nothing to protect his family from their greatest trials and suffering, because he will be dead and gone when that hour comes. If there's no sword to pierce Joseph's soul, there's surely a hammer to beat against it.

Simeon's somber words reminded the Holy Family all too clearly that their own mission was, like Jesus, only in its infancy. The Holy Family's mission was just beginning, and much suffering lay ahead of them before they could say their own *Nunc Dimittis* ("Lord, now lettest thou thy servant depart in peace"). But Joseph's own *Nunc Dimittis* would be bittersweet. Even though Joseph, the patron of a happy death, would die in peace, surrounded by Jesus and Mary, he must have wept to leave them just as Jesus' hour was approaching. God was dismissing His most faithful servant, just when that servant most wanted to serve. Now we ask to consecrate ourselves to the Holy Family in order that we may unite ourselves to the ones who were united in their suffering at the Cross. We do this in hope that we, too, may say our own *Nunc Dimittis* as we depart this life and may be welcomed into the next by the Holy Family.

Pray the Litany of the Holy Family (page 207).

DAY 22

Holy Family, persecuted and exiled to a foreign country, have pity on us

> Now when [the wise men] had departed, behold, an angel of the Lord appeared to Joseph in a dream and said, "Rise, take the child and his mother, and flee to Egypt, and remain there till I tell you; for Herod is about to search for the child, to destroy him." And he rose and took the child and his mother by night, and departed to Egypt, and remained there until the death of Herod. This was to fulfil what the Lord had spoken by the prophet, "Out of Egypt have I called my son."
>
> — Mt 2:13–15

Throughout His life, Jesus seemed to place a high premium on people's faith in Him and their willingness to drop everything and follow Him — those who seem to instantly comprehend His divine mission and act on it. We see this when Jesus calls the apostles. To St. Peter and St. Andrew, Jesus says, "'Follow me, and I will make you fishers of men.' *Immediately* they left their nets and followed him" (Mt 4:19–20, emphasis added). We see this first, however, in Mary and Joseph's immediate responses to their Son's divine mission.

"As he said this, a woman in the crowd raised her voice and said to him, 'Blessed is the womb that bore you, and the breasts that you sucked!' But [Jesus] said, 'Blessed rather are those who hear the word of God and keep it!'" (Lk 11:27–28). Many erroneously take this as a slight to the Blessed Mother, but Jesus is pointing to the greater reason for Mary's blessed status than her physical motherhood. She heard the Word of God and bound her entire life to it. She heard and acted immediately and unwaveringly. So, too, did St. Joseph.

The angel "said, 'Rise, take the child and his mother, and flee to Egypt … for Herod is about to search for the child, to destroy him'" (Mt 2:13). That was all Joseph needed to be told. He immediately took his wife and child into Egypt and did this without any question. Jesus will later say, likely with the memory of Joseph glimmering in His eye, "No one who puts his hand to the plow and looks back is fit for the kingdom of God" (Lk 9:62). For this reason, the esteemed Josephologist Fr. Francis Filas once noted, "We can well understand, then, with what joy the eyes of the Babe looked up at St. Joseph and saw him obeying promptly without a word of complaint or questioning."[1]

Hunted by the Devil

> Don't let the many snares of this infernal beast frighten you. Jesus, who is always with you, and who will fight with and for you, will never permit you to be tricked and overcome.[2]
>
> — St. Padre Pio

The quote above from St. Padre Pio can be very comforting in the midst of a spiritual battle. Jesus is always there to "fight with and for you." Your best friend is the strongest kid on the block, in the whole school, and even the whole universe for that matter. What do you have to fear? Nothing. But what if, instead of being the strongest kid in the whole universe, he was, for a time, the weakest and most vulnerable? A baby. Further, what if the roles were reversed? Instead of your friend constantly defending you, you now must defend him. This was the challenge that God placed before St. Joseph. Before Jesus can fight for you — and for all the universe — you must first fight for Jesus. Also, Jesus going from strong to weak and you going from defended to defender are not the only reversals. There's one more. Your enemy is suddenly the biggest kid on the block, and he's also the commander of all the bullies in town. Imagine the plight of St. Joseph. Imagine being personally hunted by the devil, by a creature that moves at the speed of thought. The devil is commanding legions of not just demons, but soldiers against you, the army of King Herod. If you fail, the devil — the great, ancient dragon — will devour your whole family.[3] And this is no ordinary family. Your wife is the Immaculate Conception, and the fate of the entire universe and all history depends on your Son. How helpless and alone St. Joseph might have felt. And yet, what a unique opportunity in the history of heroes and heroism.

And yet, even in Jesus' apparently great vulnerability, He was still always with St. Joseph and Mary. We return to the words of St. Padre Pio above: "Jesus, who is always with you, and who will fight with and for you, will never permit you to be tricked and overcome." Jesus never left their side — as a baby, swaddled up tight, He couldn't have left them even if He tried. His mere presence, mysteriously, means the Holy Family is never tricked or overcome, despite the apparently overwhelming odds. His presence, much less His infinite strength, may not always be apparent; and yet He is always there. In this, Jesus gives us the same opportunity for courage and heroism that He gave Mary and Joseph.

Hold tight to Jesus, just as the Holy Family did, as you would hold tightly to a babe clinging to your breast. The Infant Jesus, even swaddled and helpless, will be your help, no matter what country or state of exile in which you find yourself. This is why we consecrate ourselves to the Holy Family. We pray, asking that Mary and Joseph will swaddle our souls up tight along with the Infant Jesus, that we can cling to the bosom of the Holy Family, and that we will never be parted from Jesus' presence.

Darkness cannot overcome Light

God gave the Holy Family an impossible task. He entrusted them with a small flame which they had to keep burning as they fled across the windswept desert. Herod, and ultimately the devil, tried to close their fists around that tiny flame. Try as they might, though, they couldn't overcome the light of Jesus. Saint Francis of Assisi once stated, "All the darkness in the world cannot extinguish the light of a single candle."[4] As Zechariah, filled with the Holy Spirit, prophesied, Jesus would "give light to those who sit in darkness and in the shadow of death, to guide our feet into the way of peace" (Lk 1:79). Not only is the light of Christ not overcome; it burns for those in darkness and the shadow of death. The light of Christ burned for the Holy Family as they fled across the desert, illuminating the torch of St. Joseph, and "guided their feet into the way of peace." The way of peace was the escape from Herod and all the other dangers present on the way to Egypt. As Jesus said, "I am the light of the world; he who follows me will not walk in darkness, but will have the light of life" (Jn 8:12). Jesus illuminated the Holy Family's path of exile, and they did not walk in darkness.

This is why we should consecrate ourselves to the Holy Family. Entrust the Holy Family with your own flame in order that they may protect it and set it ablaze. Let the light of Christ burning within you be increased by St. Joseph and magnified by the Virgin Mary. As St. Josemaría Escrivá said, "Don't let your life be sterile. Be useful. Blaze a trail. Shine forth with the light of your faith … and light up all the ways of the earth with the fire of Christ that you carry in your heart."[5]

As once Joseph the Patriarch was sold into slavery in Egypt, now again the New Joseph is exiled to Egypt with the Holy Family. Joseph the Patriarch stored up and protected the grain of Egypt during famine so that Egypt could feed the world with bread. Now, again, St. Joseph is protecting the Bread of Life in order that, one day, Jesus can feed the world with His flesh. The flame of Christ, though exiled and hidden for a time in Egypt, will one day emerge as a raging fire to destroy the devil. Let the Holy Family increase and magnify the flame within you as well, in order that the Eucharist might burn brightly within you. As St. John Chrysostom said, "The Eucharist is a fire that inflames us, that like lions breathing fire, we may retire from the altar being made terrible to the devil."[6]

Overcome Evil with Good

Egypt was a land full of idols. If something moved in Egypt, the Egyptians hoisted it onto a pedestal and worshipped it. They worshipped dogs, crocodiles, cats, frogs, birds, goats, the sun, and even the Nile River. This was the reason for the Ten Plagues of Egypt. God was cleansing the land of its idols and false gods. Unfortunately, because even God's people had been slowly corrupted by the demons that the Egyptians worshipped as gods, God freed the Israelites from their bondage to idols by putting the false gods of Egypt to death one by one. Through Moses, God turned the Nile to blood, thus slaughtering Hapi, the god of the Nile, by showing His superiority to the false idol. This was the first plague of Egypt. The second was the plague of frogs, associated with Heqet, the goddess of fertility, rebirth, and childbirth. And so on, and so on. The Egyptians worshipped the sun as the god Ra, so in the ninth plague God sent darkness across the land of Egypt for three days.

The Patriarch Joseph was exiled to Egypt. This set in motion a chain of events that ultimately resulted in Moses destroying the idols of Egypt. In the same way, the New Joseph leads the Holy Family into exile in Egypt; and the New Moses, Jesus, again destroys the idols of that nation. The Holy Family enters Egypt that the coming of Jesus might again cleanse it from idolatry and consecrate it to the true God. The New Moses will not only destroy the idols but also illuminate Egypt with a legacy of sanctity. Pope St. Leo the Great describes this: "Then also the Saviour was brought to Egypt, in order that a nation given up to ancient errors might now be signed for salvation nigh to come, for hidden grace, and that she which had not yet cast out superstition from her mind might receive truth as her guest."[7] This is also the fulfillment of a prophecy from Isaiah: "An oracle concerning Egypt. Behold, the Lord is riding on a swift cloud and comes to Egypt; and the idols of Egypt will tremble at his presence, and the heart of the Egyptians will melt within them" (Is 19:1). Various ancient texts describe the idols shattering or even bowing in supplication when the Holy Family entered Egypt.[8] The presence of the Holy Family had a lasting impact on the Egyptians, who came to know, worship, and love the true God directly through the Holy Family. Faith and sanctity so flourished in Egypt that it produced the Desert Fathers: St. Paul of Thebes, the first hermit; St. Anthony of Egypt, "and those crowds of monks and anchorites who emulated the life of angels upon earth, as is seen in Eusebius, [St.] Jerome, Palladius, [St.] Athanasius, and the lives of the Fathers."[9] Saint John Chrysostom would even say that Jesus converted Egypt into a paradise: "Heaven does not shine so brightly with the various choirs of the stars as Egypt is illuminated by its innumerable habitations of monks and virgins."[10]

This is why we consecrate ourselves to the Holy Family. We pray that the same driving wind of sanctity that once swept through Egypt and smashed its idols to pieces would also enter our own hearts. We pray that at the coming of Christ all our idols would also be destroyed: pride, lust, wrath, greed, gluttony, envy, and sloth. Not only that, we pray that the desert of shattered idols may become a fertile place for sanctity to take root and grow.

Pray the Litany of the Holy Family (page 207).

DAY 23

Holy Family, hidden and unknown in Nazareth, have pity on us

> Tell all the congregation of Israel that on the tenth day of this month they shall take every man a lamb according to their fathers' houses, a lamb for a household ... Your lamb shall be without blemish, a male a year old; you shall take it from the sheep or from the goats; and you shall keep it until the fourteenth day of this month, when the whole assembly of the congregation of Israel shall kill their lambs in the evening.
>
> — Ex 12:3, 5–6

From the 10th until the 14th day of the month — five days — the Israelites would keep the Passover lamb in their homes with them. Imagine bringing this 1-year-old lamb into your home for five days, then having to slaughter it. While our modern notion of keeping pets might seem strange to a first-century Jew, there would still be a sense in which the Passover lamb became a member of the family during this time of inspection before its slaughter.

Now, think about the Lamb of God, Jesus. Think about the hidden years when the Lamb of God lived in the humble home of Nazareth. After the finding of Jesus in the Temple during Passover, instead of remaining in the Temple, He "went down with them and came to Nazareth, and was obedient to them; and his mother kept all these things in her heart. And Jesus increased in wisdom and in stature, and in favor with God and man" (Lk 2:51–52).

The Lamb of God was truly a member of the household of Nazareth. But think also of Mary, keeping "all these things in her heart." Every year for Passover, the Holy Family, either by itself or together with relatives, would have brought a Passover lamb into their household. It was a living sign of Jesus' future death and sacrifice. Every single Passover lamb slaughtered by Israel — millions and millions of lambs — pointed to Jesus, the Lamb of God, and His slaughter on the Cross. How that unblemished lamb and its annual slaughter must have pierced the Hearts of the Blessed Mother and St. Joseph!

The Interior Life

> You must not think of the soul as insignificant and petty but as an interior world containing the number of beautiful mansions you have seen; as indeed it should, since in the center of the soul there is a mansion reserved for God himself.[1]
>
> — St. Teresa of Ávila

Jesus' hidden life in Nazareth is the blueprint for the interior life. The day-to-day intimacy that Mary and Joseph experienced with Jesus is the ultimate goal of every mystic, which is the most perfect interior union with Jesus. We are adopted into the Holy Family so that we can experience this family life as well.

Make your heart into the hidden place where Jesus comes to rest. Saint Faustina said that "Jesus loves hidden souls. A hidden flower is the most fragrant." She strove to make the interior of her soul "a resting place for the Heart of Jesus." [2] So should we. How do we do this? Consecrate your heart and your interior life to the Holy Family. We ask Jesus through Mary and Joseph to remodel our hearts after the model home of Nazareth.

Your Vocation

Think of the vocations of Joseph and Mary, of man and woman, father and mother, carpenter and homemaker. They modeled for us how our vocations must be founded on a life hidden with the Child Jesus. Saint Faustina was often found with the Child Jesus in her own interior life. The Blessed

Mother obtained for St. Faustina the grace of an interior life in a way that deepened and enlivened her vocation: "*My daughter, I shall obtain for you the grace of an interior life which will be such that, without ever leaving that interior life, you will be able to carry out all your external duties with even greater care. Dwell with Him continuously in your own heart. He will be your strength.*"[3] The interior life is not just for when you're alone in prayer. This intimacy with Jesus stays with you, whatever your vocation. As St. Teresa of Ávila said, "Even when we are in the kitchen, our Lord is moving among the pots and the pans."[4]

Your first vocation is to make your dwelling in the Holy Family. Everything flows from this wellspring. Finding your vocation is not about deciding between being a monk or banker, a mom or a mother superior. It's first and foremost about finding Jesus. You can't "find yourself" without first finding Jesus.

Pope St. John Paul II said that it "is essential for us to understand that Jesus has a specific task in life for each and every one of us. Each one of us is hand-picked, called by name — by Jesus!"[5] Every one of us has a divine vocation. First and foremost, it's to be a member of the Holy Family.

Seek First the Kingdom of God

> Consider the lilies of the field, how they grow; they neither toil nor spin; yet I tell you, even Solomon in all his glory was not arrayed like one of these. But if God so clothes the grass of the field, which today is alive and tomorrow is thrown into the oven, will he not much more clothe you, O men of little faith? Therefore do not be anxious, saying, "What shall we eat?" or "What shall we drink?" or "What shall we wear?" For the Gentiles seek all these things; and your heavenly Father knows that you need them all. But seek first his kingdom

> and his righteousness, and all these things shall be yours as well.
>
> — Mt 6:28–33

Jesus tells us not to focus on the exteriors, what we will eat or drink or wear. Focus instead, He says, on the interior life, because exteriors can be distracting and even deceiving. The Holy House of Nazareth, surely among the humblest of homes, was actually the greatest of interior castles. It was a mansion of graces. It was a vault for the greatest treasures. Our senses would have utterly failed us to look upon it. Solomon, in all his glory, his temple and palaces, could not have matched the glory contained in this most simple of homes. Just as Jesus would disguise His own Body, Blood, Soul, and Divinity as simple bread, so, too, was the Kingdom of God hidden within that humble home.

In our pursuit of the interior life, we find in the humble home of Nazareth — living day in and day out in the presence of the Holy Family — that we need to be willing to sacrifice all exterior distractions. The rich young man was called to do exactly this. Jesus tells him, "One thing you still lack. Sell all that you have and distribute to the poor, and you will have treasure in heaven; and come, follow me" (Lk 18:22). If you want the treasures of Heaven, detach yourself from the treasures of earth. Attach yourself first to the treasures of Heaven. This priority will order all things rightly. Follow Jesus first, and everything else will follow. The true, the good, and the beautiful which will follow from this priority cannot be purchased, achieved, or even equaled through exterior means.

This includes not only detachment from exterior goods and pursuits, but also detachment from one's own life. To have life, we must be willing to surrender our life to Jesus. Saint Teresa of Ávila describes how this represents an exchange of our anxieties for peace, our slavery for freedom:

> I repeat that this consists mainly or entirely in our ceasing to care about ourselves and our own pleasures, for the least that anyone who is beginning to serve the Lord truly can offer him is his life. Once he has surrendered his will to him, what has he to fear? It is evident that if he is a true religious and a real man of prayer and aspires to the enjoyment of Divine consolations, he must not [turn back or] shrink from desiring to die and suffer martyrdom for his sake … and so we must not set store by anything that comes to an end, least of all by life, since not a day of it is secure. Who, if he thought that each hour might be his last, would not spend it in labour?[6]

Consecration to the Holy Family is surrendering one's exterior life in exchange for the interior life of Nazareth. The little home of Nazareth is the "pearl of great price" (Mt 13:46, NABRE). This pearl is worth everything, all that you have and are, your very life. The Holy Family's door stands wide open, yet any of these things, if not sold or relinquished, will bar the door against you.

Pray the Litany of the Holy Family (page 207).

DAY 24

Holy Family, faithful in observance of divine laws, have pity on us

> And he went down with them and came to Nazareth, and was obedient to them; and his mother kept all these things in her heart. And Jesus increased in wisdom and in stature, and in favor with God and man.
>
> — Lk 2:51–52

This is an extraordinary statement. God was obedient to Mary and Joseph! God made Himself subject to man! Both sides of this equation are unbelievable. As St. Bernard of Clairvaux said, "Choose which you will most admire, the gracious condescension of the son, or the surpassing dignity of the mother [and father]. Both are amazing; both are miraculous."[1]

We will discuss today obedience to the law which flows from the heart. As we hear in the great cry of Psalm 51:10, "Create in me a clean heart, O God, and put a new and right spirit within me." We ask for the grace to love the law of God with a heart and spirit ordered to Him and His Holy Spirit. In this pursuit, we turn our own hearts to the most precious Hearts of the Holy Family: the Sacred Heart of Jesus, the Immaculate Heart of Mary, and the Most Chaste Heart of Joseph.

Divine Law

The Divine Law is revealed by God. Pope St. John Paul II said, "*What man is and what he must do becomes clear as soon as God reveals himself*."[2] The Ten Commandments, called the Decalogue for the "ten words," begins with a statement of God revealing Himself. The Decalogue begins, "I am the Lord your God, who brought you out of the land of Egypt, out of the house of bondage" (Ex 20:2). In these "ten words" of the Covenant with Israel, and throughout the Old Testament,

God reveals Himself as the One who alone is good. God also reveals Himself as the model for moral action: "You shall be holy; for I the Lord your God am holy" (Lev 19:2). God gives us the Divine Law, as Pope St. John Paul II noted, "to restore man's original and peaceful harmony with the Creator and with all creation, and, what is more, to draw him into his divine love."[3] God promises great rewards for obeying His Divine Law: "I will give you your rains in their season, and the land shall yield its increase, and the trees of the field shall yield their fruit … and you shall eat your bread to the full" (Lev 26:4–5). And, as the greatest reward of all, God promises that He will draw us to Himself, and we will become partakers of His presence: "I will walk among you, and will be your God, and you shall be my people" (Lev 26:12).

The Holy Family dutifully followed the Divine Law, and their reward was the greatest of all, the first fruits of the plentiful harvest that was to come. God promised that He would walk among us, and He truly walked among Mary and Joseph. God was among them longer than anyone else. What man or woman has known God's presence better or shared in it more than Mary and Joseph? For 30 years, God was hidden among them. God's own presence — His tiny beating Heart — lived within Mary bodily for nine months. The same ten words of the Decalogue became the Word made flesh within Mary. Mary and Joseph were surely His people, too. They were made the family of God, the Holy Family. We consecrate ourselves to the Holy Family in order that we might achieve harmony with God, not just by following the ten words of the Divine Law, but by having the Word live within us, too, directing us to obedience from within. We consecrate ourselves to the Holy Family in order that God's presence may live and abide in us, and that we may abide with Him in the Holy House of Nazareth as His own family with Mary and Joseph.

Natural Law

God's law, His Word living within us, is the source of natural law. God created man and ordered him, according to Pope St. John Paul II, "with wisdom and love to his final end, through the law which is inscribed in his heart."[4] This is the natural law. Natural law, as St. Thomas Aquinas notes, "is nothing other than the light of understanding infused in us by God, whereby we understand what must be done and what must be avoided."[5] God gave this light of natural law to man at creation, and it was restored through Christ.

All of creation began with natural law inscribed into its being, its very nature. God began to restore all creation, all human nature, and thus natural law, through His chosen people, Israel. God did this by making a covenant with Israel, and the Law of the covenant was the ten words, the Ten Commandments (see also Ex 20). God called Israel to be His "own possession among all peoples, … a holy nation" (Ex 19:5–6), a nation ordered to the natural law through the Ten Commandments. Through Israel, God would radiate His Holiness to all peoples.[6] The gift of the "ten words" was a promise and a sign pointing to the New Covenant, when the Word of God would be made flesh in order to write the New Law on the flesh of the human heart (see also Jer 31:31–34). The human heart had been disfigured by sin, but God would "create in us a clean heart," "a new heart," for in it would dwell "a new spirit," the Spirit of God (see also Jer 17:1; Ps 51:10; Ez 36:24–28).

This is why we consecrate ourselves to the Holy Family. We ask not only that God will give us clean and pure hearts; we ask for new hearts as well. Specifically, we ask for the Immaculate Heart of Mary, the Most Chaste Heart of St. Joseph, and, most especially, for the Sacred Heart of Jesus. We consecrate ourselves to these three Hearts, asking for them to be our hearts, in order that the law be written perfectly in our hearts. As St. Augustine says, "For a clean heart to be created, the unclean one must be crushed."[7] We ask for the Hearts of the Holy Family, which were pierced, though clean and precious, to replace our hearts crushed by sin.

Holy Matrimony

The Old and New Covenants are family covenants. It's hard to overstate the importance of this distinction, especially as we meditate on the Holy Family. We're saved through the New Covenant, because we're adopted into the covenant family of Jesus. Covenants make unrelated people into family. Think about the covenant of matrimony. The previously unrelated spouses become husband and wife, a family — the two become one. In the Holy Family, we see the perfect wedding of the New Covenant and the marriage covenant, Holy Matrimony. It could even be said that the fruit of the marriage covenant of Joseph and Mary is the New Covenant.[8]

Holy Matrimony is, therefore, essential to the salvation of mankind. This is why the devil attacks it. In our present time, we are witnessing what the visionary of Our Lady of Fatima, Sr. Lucia, described as "the final battle between the Lord and the kingdom of Satan [over] Marriage and the Family."[9] As many nations began legalizing divorce in the late 19th century, Pope Leo XIII became keenly aware that this final battle was breaking out and spoke prophetically on marriage and divorce. He recalled the fundamental role of the family as the organic cell of civil society: "[The family,] sadly undermined in these our times, cannot possibly be restored to its due dignity, save by those laws under which it was established in the Church by her Divine Founder Himself."[10] In the encyclical *Arcanum* (1880), the first pontifical document on marriage, he spoke on the evils that would follow divorce:

> [M]utual kindness is weakened; deplorable inducements to unfaithfulness are supplied; harm is done to the education and training of children; occasion is afforded for the breaking up of homes; the seeds

> of dissension are sown among families; the dignity of womanhood is lessened and brought low, and women run the risk of being deserted after having ministered to the pleasures of men. Since, then, nothing has such power to lay waste families and destroy the mainstay of kingdoms as the corruption of morals, it is easily seen that divorces are in the highest degree hostile to the prosperity of families and States, springing as they do from the depraved morals of the people, and, as experience shows us, opening out a way to every kind of evil-doing in public and in private life.[11]

Many of the evils of society we now experience can be explained in terms of these prophetic lines from Pope Leo XIII. The challenges now facing us seem almost insurmountable. And yet, Sister Lucia, she said, "Don't be afraid, because anyone who works for the sanctity of Marriage and the Family will always be fought and opposed in every way, because this is the decisive issue."[12] This is why we consecrate ourselves to the Holy Family. The Holy Family is the ultimate weapon for defending the sanctity of marriage and the family. The restoration of the law requires the restoration of the family, and the Holy Family is, from all time, the restorer of the covenant of the family.

Pray the Litany of the Holy Family (page 207).

DAY 25

Holy Family, perfect model of the Christian family, have pity on us

> [The liturgical feast of the Holy Family] invites us to contemplate the *Holy Family of Nazareth*, a wonderful model of human and supernatural virtues for all Christian families. Let us meditate on the mystery of this unique family: we can find in it values and teachings which today are more indispensable than ever to give human society sound and stable foundations.[1]
>
> — Pope St. John Paul II

Pope St. John Paul II directs us to the Holy Family as the model of virtues for all families and the antidote to an increasingly anti-family society. The Holy Family is the ultimate model for the family, the "Domestic Church." The Gospel values and virtues that define the family — prayer, understanding, respect, discipline, sacrifice, work, and charity — are drawn from the Holy Family.[2] Pope St. John Paul also invites us to "[contemplate] this admirable model, [from which] the Church draws the values to hold up to the women and men of all times and all cultures."[3] The Holy Family isn't just an image for Christmastime; it's the foundation of all families. The Holy Family shows us the meaning of Emmanuel, "God with us."

The Model Family

These values and virtues, modeled so perfectly by the Holy Family, can only be understood in terms of Emmanuel, "God with us." Some of the most important values and virtues, as listed by Pope St. John Paul II, are prayer, understanding, respect, discipline, sacrifice, work, and charity. Think about these in terms of Christ being physically present in the Holy House of Nazareth. God is with the interior life of that Holy

House in a literal way. In terms of prayer, the Holy Family doesn't pray to God as to some remote, abstract concept. God abides bodily in the home, as He should in our homes. In terms of understanding, God certainly, intimately understands the day-to-day struggles and joys of the Holy Family because He's a member of it. Prayerfully consider each of these values in terms of Jesus' physical presence in Nazareth. Even reflect on discipline, for Jesus "was obedient to them" (Lk 2:51).

Meditate, as well, on the values of sacrifice and work. (The great respect they had, specifically the mutual respect that existed between the members of the Holy Family, will be discussed tomorrow.) All their work and sacrifice, all the daily family and work struggles, were performed directly for Jesus. Every swing of St. Joseph's hammer and swish of Mary's broom was done for Jesus. Every jar of water that she drew from the well was for Jesus, the "spring of living water" (see also Jn 4:14).

Lastly, think of charity, which is working together lovingly for the common good. The good works of the Holy Family didn't end at the holy doorstep of Nazareth; they extend to the entire universe and all time. Love (charity) truly does make the world go round. Their good works and the fruits of their charity ripple into eternity.

God's actual, physical presence in the home of the Holy Family gives sublime new meaning to these values. The purpose of having the Holy Family as a model isn't to show how different it is from us, but rather how alike it is. God is physically present within us and our families, too, as much as He was at home in Nazareth. As St. Augustine says, "The Lord is closer to us than we are to ourselves."[4] This is why we consecrate ourselves to the Holy Family in order that we may live, work, and sacrifice in Jesus' own presence. The Holy Family models all these values and virtues, not as remote, abstract concepts, but as lived realities, lived in the direct presence of Jesus.

Prayerful Parents

Part of prayer is training ourselves to remain in the presence of Jesus, that in praying to Him we may spend time with Him. Think of the effortless way the Holy Family prayed in Jesus' presence. He was right there in their midst and beside them, day-by-day, every day.

The Holy Family is the model of remaining in prayer in Jesus' presence. Certainly, Mary and Joseph were uniquely prayerful parents. However, they're not our models because their level of prayerfulness is unobtainable for us. Rather, they bring us to Him. Mary and Joseph teach us that we, too, can live always in Jesus' presence. This is an encouraging thought. The Holy Family isn't far from us, but very near. They are, after all, our family.

The Church has recognized and even canonized many sets of prayerful parents, such as St. Thérèse of Lisieux's parents, Sts. Louis and Zélie Martin. The Martins were deeply devoted to the Holy Family. Pope St. John Paul II wrote the following in his "Letter to Families": "*The Holy Family is the beginning of countless other holy families.* The Council [Vatican II] recalled that holiness is the vocation of all the baptized. In our age, as in the past, there is no lack of witnesses to the 'gospel of the family,' even if they are not well known or have not been proclaimed saints by the Church."[5] Your consecration to the Holy Family will help carry this perfect model throughout the world. The Holy Family is the seed that sanctifies families as it grows, creating prayerful parents and virtuous children. The Martin family, like a branch growing from Jesus' family tree, thus became a model of the Holy Family able to reach out to others.

Again, this is the meaning of the Holy House of Nazareth — Nazareth, which means both "branch" and "consecration."[6] As a branch of this Holy Family tree, we are grafted by covenant and Baptism onto the "true vine" which is Jesus (Jn 15:1). As Jesus instructs us, "Abide in me, and I in you.

As the branch cannot bear fruit by itself, unless it abides in the vine, neither can you, unless you abide in me" (Jn 15:4). If we abide with Jesus in Nazareth, we will receive life abundantly and bear abundant fruit for others as well.

Virtuous Children

As mentioned in the previous section, Jesus instructs us, "Abide in me, and I in you. As the branch cannot bear fruit by itself, unless it abides in the vine, neither can you, unless you abide in me" (Jn 15:4). This great fruit is all the gifts of the Holy Spirit, as well as good works, both Spiritual and Corporal Works of Mercy. One of the principal fruits, however, is virtuous children. The Holy Family is the model of all virtues, and the Holy House of Nazareth is also the school of virtue.

In *Breve Neminem Fugit*, Pope Leo XIII sets out the Holy Family as the universal model of virtue and holiness:

> When God in His mercy determined to accomplish the work of man's renewal, which same had so many long ages awaited, He appointed and ordained this work on such wise that its very beginning might shew to the world the august spectacle of a Family which was known to be divinely constituted; that therein all men might behold a perfect model, as well of domestic life as of every virtue and pattern of holiness: for such indeed was the Holy Family of Nazareth.[7]

What should we base society on? What's the blueprint for civilization? We're told above that it's the Holy Family. To flourish, domestic society must be based on the Domestic Church, and the Domestic Church is founded on the Holy Family. Saint José Manyanet, called the "Apostle of the Holy Family," explained it this way: "Nazareth, God's design for the family: To make a Nazareth in every home, that is, to make every family become another Holy Family."[8] To this end, St. José Manyanet recommended that families frequently spend time in adoration before the Blessed Sacrament. To St. José Manyanet, this was a perfect way to model the perfect family: bring Jesus bodily into your daily family life.[9]

Pray the Litany of the Holy Family (page 207).

DAY 26

Holy Family, center of peace and concord, have pity on us

> To gather round the Bethlehem grotto contemplating there the Holy Family, enables us to appreciate the gift of *family intimacy* in a special way, and spurs us to offer human warmth and concrete solidarity in those unfortunately numerous situations which, for various reasons, lack peace, harmony, in a word, lack "family."[1]
>
> — Pope St. John Paul II

The peace and concord of the Holy Family are extraordinary, given the infinite gulf that exists between parents and Child. The union of God and man in Jesus creates the strangest, most extraordinary, and most beautiful family dynamics. This is because the parents were both created by their Child. Likewise, the Child, who is God, is the Creator of His parents. The peace and concord that exist preeminently in the Holy Family are all the more extraordinary in light of this seemingly impossible configuration. This peace and concord flow from the mutual respect of father, mother, and Child. This impossibility is only made possible through God's infinite love for His children.

One of the principal Gospel virtues taught in the family is mutual respect. Pope St. John Paul II listed mutual respect as one of the greatest values modeled by the Holy Family: "Recollection and prayer, mutual understanding and respect, personal discipline and community asceticism and a spirit of sacrifice, work and solidarity are typical features that make the family of Nazareth a model for every home."[2]

Mutual Respect

Mutual respect is one of the most striking features of the Holy Family, especially when one considers the extraordinary strangeness of it: The father and head is the least in dignity. Typically in salvation history, the father, the patriarch, is accorded the place of greatest honor. Not so with the Holy Family. The father falls to a distant third when the mother is the Immaculata, the woman prophesied to defeat Satan from Genesis to Revelation, and the Son is God Himself.

However, this is why the Holy Family is the finest — and by far most extraordinary — model for mutual respect. The father, though least in dignity, still serves as head of the Holy Family. The respect given by the parents, Mary and Joseph, to their Son, almost goes without saying. Nevertheless, never before in history and never again will the parents' respect for their child actually be mandated by the First and Second Commandments! In the Holy Family, the parents' respect for their Child is actually elevated to worship, the worship reserved to God alone. A child's respect for his parents, however, is always mandated by the Ten Commandments, namely the Fourth Commandment: "Honor your father and your mother" (Dt 5:16).[3] The Hebrew word used for "honor" in the Fourth Commandment hints at an elevated sense of honor, more akin to "glory" or "veneration."[4] This also makes the order of the Holy Family very strange and the resulting peace and concord unsurpassable. Only in the uniqueness of the Holy Family do we find an instance of God Himself being bound by the Ten Commandments to honor and venerate some of His own creatures. This is an extraordinary statement. It's well stated by St. Bernard of Clairvaux:

> God, Whom the powers and principalities obey, was subject to Mary. And not only to Mary, but to Joseph also for Mary's sake. Consider, then, and choose which you will most admire, the gracious condescension of the son, or the surpassing dignity of the mother. Both are amazing; both are miraculous. That a God should obey a woman is humility

> without example; that a woman should command the Son of God is a dignity without parallel.[5]

There has never been such an immense gulf between the respect owed by the natural order of things, and what God willingly submits Himself to. Through an act of familial love, God bridges the infinite gulf which separates us from Him. This infinity-spanning love for His own creation is ultimately manifested in Jesus' willingness to die for us on the Cross, "while we were yet sinners" (Rom 5:8).

And yet, we, too, are called to be members of this most extraordinary of families. The immense mutual respect shown within the Holy Family should make us humbly consider this invitation — an invitation of infinite graciousness. Consecration to, and adoption into, the Holy Family is the greatest of honors. Not only does this family covenant spare us from eternal damnation; we are also being invited to a seat of immeasurable honor: blood brothers of Jesus and true children of Mary and Joseph. We, too, will share in the boundless mutual respect of the Holy Family.

The Domestic Church

The center of every home, every Domestic Church, should be peace and concord. The peace and concord of society flow from the home. Likewise, great unrest in society flows from great unrest in the home. The answer to this problem is putting the Holy Family at the center of family life. Dropping the Holy Family into the center of a home has the opposite effect of dropping a stone into calm water. When the Holy Family is dropped into a home, waves of peace and concord spread outward from this new center. The waves are smoothing instead of rippling. Peace and concord spread outward from house to house, family to family. Tensions and anxieties relax as people grow more concerned with Jesus than material distractions.

Why is the Holy Family a center of peace and concord? What qualities make the Holy Family the ideal "Domestic

Church"? Pope St. John Paul II described these qualities while speaking about the Holy House of Loreto, which was the house of the Virgin Mary's Annunciation and later home to the Holy Family:

> The memory of the hidden life of Nazareth evokes very concrete issues that are close to the experience of every man and every woman; it awakens the sense of the sanctity of the family, highlighting a whole world of values, today so threatened, such as fidelity, respect for life, education of children and prayer, which Christian families can rediscover within the walls of the Holy House, the first and exemplary domestic church in history.[6]

The family naturally cultivates these values of life and education of children. However, when a home is elevated to a Domestic Church in the image of the Holy Family, supernatural virtues take root as well, watered by sanctity and prayer and the presence of Jesus. As Pope St. John Paul instructs us, "[E]very Christian family is called to be a small '*domestic church*' that must shine with the Gospel virtues."[7] So formed, Christian families naturally interlock to form a society, a community of life and love, all radiating from the Holy Family, the center of peace and concord.

Perseverance

Making a home takes persistence. Disrepair wants to ruin the house, and disorder wants to rot it from within. It helps to have a good carpenter on hand. This is why we look to the Holy Family as a center of peace and concord. For a house to avoid even natural decay and collapse, a family needs perseverance. For a family to avoid collapse, supernatural perseverance is needed. Many more families are formed today than ultimately succeed in marriage. This is why we need the Holy Family. As St. Josemaría Escrivá said, "To begin is for everyone. To persevere is for saints."[8] As the family is increasingly under attack, all of us must set our standards higher. We need the Holy Family to make us saints. The world needs you to persevere like the saints, to lift more, perhaps a lot more, than previous generations did. You're being asked to do this during a time of great sin and distraction but don't fear. "Where sin increased, grace abounded all the more" (Rom 5:20). Though the burdens are perhaps heavier than they were for past generations, we have greater help in lifting them. The Holy Family is here to help you.

Take heart! "Count it all joy, my brethren, when you meet various trials, for you know that the testing of your faith produces steadfastness. And let steadfastness have its full effect, that you may be perfect and complete, lacking in nothing" (Jas 1:2–4). Who was tested more than the Holy Family? Who endured more, persevered more? For the Holy Family, this "steadfastness [had] its full effect." The Holy Family was perfect, complete, and lacking in nothing. This is why it's the center of peace and concord. As St. Augustine says, "You have made us for yourself, O Lord, and our hearts are restless until they rest in you."[9] The Hearts of the Holy Family — the Sacred Heart, the Immaculate Heart, and the Most Chaste Heart — aren't restless. They're at peace because they rest in the Lord. In the Holy Family, the Sacred Heart itself rests in the arms of Mary and Joseph. If you seek rest, go to the Holy House of Nazareth — this is the place where all of us and our families can find peace and rest.

Pray the Litany of the Holy Family *(page 207).*

DAY 27

Holy Family, whose protector is a model of paternal care, have pity on us

> The divine house, which Joseph governed with patriarchal power, contained the seeds of the incipient Church. The most holy Virgin, being the mother of Jesus Christ, is also the mother of all Christians, because she begot them on Mount Calvary, amid the supreme sufferings of the Redeemer; and Jesus Christ is also like the first-born of Christians who, by adoption and redemption, are his brothers. In all this is to be seen the reason why the Most Blessed Patriarch [St. Joseph] has, as if for a singular reason, entrusted to himself the multitude of Christians of which the Church is composed, that is, that innumerable family spread throughout the world, over which he, being the spouse of Mary and the father of Jesus Christ, enjoys a sort of paternal authority. It is reasonable, therefore, and very much in keeping with the dignity of Blessed Joseph that, as he was once accustomed to defend the Family of Nazareth in everything it needed, so now he should protect and defend the Church of Christ with heavenly patronage.[1]
>
> — Pope Leo XIII

The Family of Nazareth is spread throughout the world. You're part of this family by adoption and Baptism. Your home is that of a beautiful, perfect family, no matter what kind of home you may have come from. When you consecrate yourself to the Holy Family, you gain the "Most Blessed Patriarch" St. Joseph as your own spiritual father. As he once defended "the Family of Nazareth in everything it needed," so now he will defend you and the Church that has grown from his family tree.

A family tree is important. It's important to know where we came from. Every family can be traced back to its origins. The seeds of the incipient Church grew and continue to grow in the house of Joseph of Nazareth. This is why St. Joseph is the Protector and Patron of the Universal Church. He was the last vestige of the family tree of King David, and Jesus was the righteous branch that shot forth and made the family tree grow anew. Nazareth, a name which can be translated as "place of the branch," reminds us that Jesus fulfilled this prophecy. It's from this new family tree of Nazareth that we all find renewed spiritual fatherhood and motherhood. Each member of the Church begins as a "living transplant of faith and the seed of doctrine, and through this daily process of transplanting," we are nurtured.[2]

Father of Jesus

> No one will ever be able to worthily praise Joseph, whom thou, O true only-begotten Son of the Eternal Father, has deigned to have for thy foster father![3]
>
> — St. Ephrem the Syrian

Saint Joseph is frequently described, according to English translations and conventions, as the "Foster Father" of Jesus. While this might come across as something merely contractual, the original Latin provides a deeper insight into St. Joseph's true role and vocation. In Latin, the title given to him to signify his role as foster father is *Filii Dei Nutricie*, which means "Nurturer of the Son of God." As you can see, the title "foster father" is a somewhat paltry translation of the original. It needs to be emphasized that St. Joseph's fatherhood was more than just a legal formality. On the contrary, his fatherhood was authoritative, affectionate, faithful, and everlasting. Regarding St. Joseph, Doctor of the Church St. Teresa of Ávila said: "Those who are devoted to prayer should, in a special manner, cherish devotion to St. Joseph. I know not how anyone can ponder on the sufferings, trials, and tribulations the Queen of Angels endured whilst caring for Jesus in his childhood, without at the same time thanking St. Joseph for the services he rendered the Divine Child and his Blessed Mother."[4]

Saint Joseph, though least in dignity, is nevertheless an incredibly important, even essential, part of the Holy Family. Likewise, holy fatherhood is an indispensable aspect of society as a whole. God established the family to be a school of love, something beautiful, delightful, and life-giving; and the devil wants to destroy it. Fatherhood, in particular, is under attack these days. The family provides order to society because the father as nurturer provides headship. How can we return to this order? The only way is to elevate the Holy Family as the model, blueprint, pillar, and foundation of the family. This is why St. Joseph is called "Pillar of the Family." In order for your home to stand unshakably on a firm foundation, you need St. Joseph. He will teach your family the importance of prayer, mutual respect, purity, honesty, forgiveness, love, and, most importantly, placing God above all things.

Chaste Spouse of Mary

> It was necessary that divine Providence should commit [Mary] to the charge and guardianship of a man absolutely pure.[5]
>
> — St. Francis de Sales

Chastity is a very important virtue. To be chaste is to have self-mastery, to be in control of your passions and sexuality. A person who exercises the virtue of chastity is not repressing or rejecting the beauty of human sexuality. Instead, chastity preserves the human heart and body for authentic self-giving. All people are called to chastity, no matter whether their vocation in life is to be a priest or layman, nun or laywoman, married spouse or single person. Chastity is the virtue that frees us from slavery to our passions. Without it, we behave like irrational animals.

Celibacy is a special form of chastity. Some men and women are called to celibacy for the sake of the Kingdom of Heaven. Saint Joseph and Mary were both chaste and celibate. Joseph was called by God to espouse a virgin consecrated to God in her mind, body, and soul. This is why we address St. Joseph in his litany as "Chaste Guardian of the Virgin." Joseph and Mary lived in a "Josephite marriage." They were truly husband and wife, though they never engaged in sexual relations. Their vocation was to be united in heart, mind, and soul, but never in body. They were both consecrated to God and sacrificed to Him a natural good in exchange for a greater good: the salvation of souls. God took this sacrifice and increased it beyond all measure by doing something truly extraordinary with this marriage of consecrated virgins: The Holy Family became the most fruitful family in human history. Through Baptism, all Christians become sons and daughters of Mary and Joseph and brothers and sisters of Jesus.

Our Spiritual Father

Saint Joseph is our spiritual father. The loving relationship between a spiritual father and a child endures forever. In other words, Jesus continues to be the Son of Joseph in Heaven. Unlike marriage, which doesn't extend into eternity, St. Joseph's spiritual fatherhood over Christ and His Mystical Body endures forever. Spiritual fatherhood, like spiritual motherhood, endures forever. Were this not the case, the Church would need to cease invoking Jesus, not only as the "Son of Joseph," but as the "Son of Mary" as well. When you are baptized into the family of Jesus and born again, you are also a child of Joseph *forever*. Saint Joseph is your "nurturer," too.

To paternally nurture someone is to do work similar to a gardener and grower. This is why "nurturer" and "foster father" are related. By being adopted into the Holy Family, we are grafted onto Joseph of Nazareth's family tree. As St. Joseph nurtured the newborn Jesus, he will nurture you and help you to grow spiritually.

In His parables, Jesus intentionally uses the imagery of trees and gardens, for Jesus is the New Adam, who brings us to the New Garden of Eden. Like in the Parable of the Sower, St. Joseph is given charge over us as God's seedlings, protecting us from the birds that would come to devour us, the harsh sun that would scorch us, and the thorns that would choke us (see also Mt 13:1–9). Saint Joseph conceals the Holy Family from the devil, so that we, as seedlings, might be transplanted to "good soil and [bring] forth grain, some a hundredfold, some sixty, some thirty" (Mt 13:8). This is why we consecrate ourselves to the Holy Family, in order that we, too, may be adopted by St. Joseph into his family and nurtured and protected by his gentle hands.

Pray the Litany of the Holy Family (page 207).

DAY 28

Holy Family, whose mother is a model of maternal diligence, have pity on us

> On that wood of the Cross her Son hangs in agony as one condemned. "He was despised and rejected by men; a man of sorrows ... he was despised, and we esteemed him not": as one destroyed (see also Is. 53:3–5). How great, how heroic then is the obedience of faith shown by Mary in the face of God's "unsearchable judgments"! How completely she "abandons herself to God" without reserve, offering the full assent of the intellect and the will to him whose "ways are inscrutable" (see also Rom. 11:33)! And how powerful too is the action of grace in her soul, how all-pervading is the influence of the Holy Spirit and of his light and power![1]
>
> — Pope St. John Paul II

What better model of maternal diligence can we seek than Mary standing at the foot of the Cross? She endured all the sufferings of her Son with unwavering faith and persisted heroically in the obedience of faith. The disciples fled, yet Mary stands, while the sword pierces both her Heart and that of her Son. It's a violence that binds them further together. By faith, the mother shares in the redeeming death of her Son. Through this faith, Mary is perfectly united with Christ in the shocking mystery of His self-emptying.

What is diligence and, in particular, "maternal diligence"? According to St. Thomas Aquinas, there are two levels of diligence. Firstly, there is sufficient diligence, which is a part of the virtue of fortitude and is defined as being ready and disposed to do what reason commands.[2] Sufficient diligence is sufficient for the individual, but there is also more than sufficient diligence. Diligence which is more than sufficient is when "man is able to make provision both for himself and for others, not only in matters necessary for salvation, but also in all things relating to human life; and such diligence as this is not in all who have grace."[3] Maternal diligence is in the category of "more than" sufficient diligence. Mary has this kind of diligence in superabundance. She is not only diligent in matters necessary for salvation; she is diligent at the very site of salvation, and she makes provision for the Savior Himself. Her presence at the Cross, now and eternally, provides not just for her Son, but for all of us, all the children of the world who are baptized into the life and death of Jesus. Because of her maternal diligence at the Cross, the Blessed Mother is now present during all our trials and difficulties. This is described beautifully by St. Thérèse of Lisieux, to whom Mary as "Our Lady of the Smile" once appeared after a period of suffering and torment. She wrote, "In trial or difficulty, I have recourse to Mother Mary, whose glance alone is enough to dissipate every fear."[4]

Mother of God

> Only in the mystery of Christ is [Mary's] mystery fully made clear. Thus has the Church sought to interpret it from the very beginning: the mystery of the Incarnation has enabled her to penetrate and to make ever clearer the mystery of the Mother of the Incarnate Word … Mary is the Mother of God (= Theotókos), since by the power of the Holy Spirit she conceived in her virginal womb and brought into the world Jesus Christ, the Son of God, who is of one being with the Father.[5]
>
> — Pope St. John Paul II

Mary, as the Mother of Christ, is united in a particular way to her children. She bore the Body of Christ in her womb, so she bore all of us who are members of the Church. The Incarnation, which united man and God in the person of Jesus, occurred within the Mother of God. As Mother of God, she also serves in a special way to unite her children to God.

The whole history of the People of God is connected to the life of the Mother of God. Mary's life was a pilgrimage of faith. This pilgrimage began, in a real sense, when God revealed her divine motherhood and Immaculate Conception after the Fall of Adam and Eve, at the very beginning of salvation history (see also Gen 3:15). This pilgrimage continued as the Blessed Virgin advanced through life, preserving her union with Christ through an unbroken journey of faith. Salvation history is the story of the "twofold bond" that unites the Mother of God to Christ and to us. We, too, as members of the ever-expanding Holy Family, join Mary in this family pilgrimage.

This is why the Virgin Mary is our model of maternal diligence. She has gone before us on pilgrimage. She has become the model of the Church in faith, charity, and perfect union with Christ. In this, Mary also becomes a model of the intimate mystery of the Church. She allows God to knit together mysteries within her inmost being, that of being both mother and virgin, daughter of God and Mother of God. Mary is a virgin and the immaculate spouse of St. Joseph. She also becomes a mother because she brings forth to a new and immortal life children who are conceived of the Holy Spirit and born of God.

Immaculate Spouse of St. Joseph

Sister Mary Wilhelmina Lancaster, a Benedictine nun from Missouri, founded the Order of the Benedictines of Mary, Queen of Apostles, and once wrote a poem about Our Lady and her love for her husband and Divine Son, Jesus. She titled the poem "Mrs. Carpenter."

> So many days'd been spent in
> building and repairing,

While Mary served and cooked,
and cooked and served;
With love and lightsome step
the family bore the load
Of daily toil. It'd been the mother's constant joy
To feed and clothe the two: her man, her Boy,
And driving nails they did
almost from morn 'til night,
While muscles strong developed
in that arm of might.

Then suddenly He said goodbye,
the shop was closed;
His father lay in peace under the hill;
And left alone she was remembering until
She heard of His arrest.
Then straight she went
To stand close by His side;
She'd be His caring mother 'til He died.

She met Him on the road carrying that log
To which He would be nailed –
How her heart quailed!
The sight gave her a start
Of tears that flowed in torrents tart;
It was the hammering, the hammering,
that broke her heart.[6]

The mystery of Mary as virgin and mother deepened in her marriage to St. Joseph. In a wondrous way, their marriage becomes infinitely fruitful, bearing countless spiritual children until the end of time. Together, Mary and Joseph bear all the members of the Church, the Mystical Body of Christ. All who are baptized into Christ's life and death become His brothers and sisters and children of Mary and Joseph. Mysteriously, these celibate spouses become a model, not just for those called to the vocation of marriage, but for all vocations.

Mary and Joseph are certainly a model for married spouses, but they're also a model for priests and religious. Pope Benedict XVI described the marital aspect of the Sacrament of Holy Orders this way: "The priest is capable of being a husband and a father according to the flesh, but by his celibacy he renounces that form of human flourishing. Out of love, he chooses to deprive himself of it in order to live as the exclusive husband of the Church."[7] As priests and men religious marry the Church, a religious sister becomes the spouse of Christ. Because of their celibacy, not in spite of it, Mary and Joseph became infinitely fruitful. Likewise, priests and men and women religious are also capable of being fruitful beyond all limitations of the flesh. A priest is the spiritual father of his entire parish. Nuns and sisters become spiritual mothers to many, even hundreds, and sometimes, like Mother Teresa (St. Teresa of Calcutta), to entire generations.

Our Spiritual Mother

The Virgin Mary is our spiritual mother. In a very real sense, Mary becomes our true mother when we are reborn in Baptism. Jesus took the opportunity to address the special role of Mary, our spiritual mother, in the Gospel of Luke: "A woman in the crowd raised her voice and said to [Jesus], 'Blessed is the womb that bore you, and the breasts that you sucked!' But he said, 'Blessed rather are those who hear the word of God and keep it!'" (Lk 11:27–28). Strangely, some interpret this as Jesus insulting Mary's motherhood. Rather, He "wishes to divert attention from motherhood understood only as a fleshly bond, in order to direct it towards those mysterious bonds of the spirit which develop from hearing and keeping God's word."[8] Elizabeth, "filled with the Holy Spirit," also addresses the unique blessedness of Mary, saying, "[B]lessed is she who believed that there would be a fulfilment of what was spoken to her from the Lord" (Lk 1:41, 45). As unique as the Virgin Birth was, being the only such birth in human history, it's Mary's faith that truly sets her apart as our spiritual mother.

Her faith can also be likened to that of Abraham, whom St. Paul calls our father in faith (see also Rom 4:12). If Abraham is our father in faith, Mary is our mother in faith. Through Abraham, Mary's own life, her pilgrimage of faith, is again mysteriously connected to all salvation history. As Pope St. John Paul II wrote, "Abraham's faith constitutes the beginning of the Old Covenant; Mary's faith at the Annunciation inaugurates the New Covenant."[9] Despite being of very advanced age and believing his wife to be barren, Abraham "in hope … believed against hope, that he should become the father of many nations" (Rom 4:18). Mary did likewise at the Annunciation, despite the apparent impossibility of her having children since she was a virgin. She declared her vow of virginity to the angel, saying, "How shall this be done, because I know not man?" (Lk 1:34, Douay-Rheims Version).[10] Her state of perpetual virginity is evident in the fact that Mary is surprised, even afraid, that the angel would announce the coming of a child to her. Most newlyweds would welcome this news. Yet Mary believed that by the power of the Most High she would become a mother, despite her virginity, and the Mother of God's Son, as well: "[T]he child to be born will be called holy, the Son of God" (Lk 1:35). This is why Mary's faith was greater than even Abraham's. He believed that God could bring life from barrenness; she believed God could bring life from virginity, from nothing.

Pray the Litany of the Holy Family (page 207).

DAY 29

Holy Family, whose Divine Child is a model of filial obedience, have pity on us

After Mary and Joseph lost Jesus and found Him again in the Temple, Scripture describes His filial obedience to His parents:

> And when they saw him they were astonished; and his mother said to him, "Son, why have you treated us so? Behold, your father and I have been looking for you anxiously." And he said to them, "How is it that you sought me? Did you not know that I must be in my Father's house?" And they did not understand the saying which he spoke to them. And he went down with them and came to Nazareth, and was obedient to them; and his mother kept all these things in her heart. And Jesus increased in wisdom and in stature, and in favor with God and man. (Lk 2:48–52)

The Gospel of Luke records a very interesting conversation within the Holy Family narrated above. In answer to Mary's question, "Son, why have you treated us so?" Jesus does something strange. He demonstrates His perfect filial obedience to both His heavenly and earthly fathers. What follows is the hidden years of Jesus within the Holy Family of Nazareth, where He "was obedient to them." This holy, filial obedience would mark all of His life. As St. Francis de Sales stated, "Obedience is a virtue of so excellent a nature, that Our Lord was pleased to mark its observance upon the whole course of his life; thus he often says, he did not come to do his own will, but that of his heavenly Father."[1] One cannot overstate the importance of holy obedience. As St. Mary Magdalene de Pazzi noted, "[A] single instant passed under simple obedience is immeasurably more valuable in the sight of God than an entire day spent in the most sublime contemplation."[2] And again from St. Francis de Sales we hear, "The Devil doesn't fear austerity but holy obedience."[3]

The Eternal Son of God

It's easy to gloss over how much Joseph and Mary suffered when they lost Jesus in the Temple. God's two holiest creatures were given a cup of sorrow directly from the hand of their loving Son, Jesus. Mary and Joseph were suddenly bereft of the light of the world, which was also their Son. No exile was difficult, no poverty depleting, no suffering counted for anything, as long as they possessed Jesus, but now He was gone. Those three days of agonizing loneliness would foreshadow Mary and the apostles' loss for the three days that Jesus lay dead in the tomb. Perhaps Jesus so arranged those three days in the Temple to prepare His mother for the future loss and console her during His three days in the tomb. When the panic of having a missing child sets in, parents' minds immediately go to the worst scenario possible. For all these holy parents knew, the time for the Redemption had arrived, and their Son was already undergoing the suffering prophesied for the Messiah. God the Father had entrusted His Son to Mary and Joseph, and they had lost Him, possibly right when His hour had come.

Why did Jesus do this and cause His parents so much pain? Not out of disrespect, but out of the depths of His love for Mary and Joseph, Jesus willed to remain in the Temple. Despite knowing the agony it would cause His parents, He exhibited a higher obedience. He willed to separate Himself from them to show us that God's will must come first, even if this priority causes pain. Jesus wished to demonstrate that His mission on earth was more important than His tenderest and closest ties. He would state this definitively years later, in the Garden of Gethsemane, making known that His mission was more important than any other consideration in His life by saying, "Father, ... not my will, but thine, be done" (Lk 22:42). Jesus was demonstrating His perfect filial obedience to His Eternal Father in Heaven. And yet, somehow almost simultaneously, He was also demonstrating His perfect filial obedience to His earthly parents as well. In Jesus, these two kinds of obedience are never at odds with one another — this is the essence of the mystery of Finding Jesus in the Temple. Jesus turned His face toward Jerusalem, where His mission of redeeming all mankind awaited Him, while also turning His face to Nazareth, where, as our perfect model, He chose a life of obscurity, prayer, and obedience amid the seemingly commonplace and ordinary.

The Son of Mary and Joseph

The passage below draws a curtain over the Finding of Jesus in the Temple, and the curtain remains drawn as we enter the hidden life of Jesus, the Son of Mary and Joseph, in Nazareth. And yet, in just this snapshot, we see the influence of both Joseph and Mary:

> And [Jesus] went down with them and came to Nazareth, and was obedient to them; and his mother kept all these things in her heart. And Jesus increased in wisdom and in stature, and in favor with God and man. (Lk 2:51–52)

We see first how Mary responds by "[keeping] all these things in her heart." She is the image of prayer and contemplation, and Jesus grows in this image. We see Joseph here as well. Joseph's name means "to increase," as Rachel, the mother of the original Joseph, prayed "to increase" her children, a prayer that would ultimately be fulfilled through Jesus (see Gen 30:24). Here we see that Jesus increased, that is, matured in wisdom, stature, and in favor with God and man in the image of Joseph. Such an increase can happen to you, too, if you entrust yourself to the paternal care of St. Joseph. Saint Bernard of Clairvaux explains this process to us: "Who and what manner of man this blessed Joseph was, you may conjecture from the name by which, a dispensation being allowed, he deserved to be so honored as to be believed and to be called the father of God. You may conjecture it from his very name, which, being interpreted, means 'Increase.'"[4]

In the same way that St. Joseph increases our virtues, Mary multiplies them. This is because Mary is the woman of the Magnificat. "[Her] soul magnifies the Lord" (Lk 1:46). We consecrate ourselves to the Holy Family in order that, as brothers and sisters of Jesus, we may enter into His hidden childhood in Nazareth. There, under their protection, St. Joseph will increase our virtues, and Mary will magnify our gifts.

Jesus, Our Brother

The Church is the family of Jesus. All the Church's members are brothers and sisters of Jesus, because the Holy Family has adopted them in a special way. Mary is the Mother of the Church, for in giving her to St. John the Apostle on Calvary, Jesus also gave her to us. Joseph is the adopted father and protector of Jesus, and thus he became the father and protector of all the Church, of everyone, everywhere. Understanding Jesus as our brother helps us better understand the very literal meaning of the following scripture: "We love, because he first loved us. If any one says, 'I love God,' and hates his brother, he is a liar; for he who does not love his brother whom he has seen, cannot love God whom he has not seen. And this commandment we have from him, that he who loves God should love his brother also" (1 Jn 4:19–21). We can't hate our brother, because Jesus is our brother. Going a step further is to submit ourselves obediently to the needs of the poor out of obedience to Jesus, who lives in the poor. As we read in the Gospel of Matthew, those whom the King is about to send to hell will answer him, "Lord, when did we see thee hungry or thirsty or a stranger or naked or sick or in prison, and did not minister to thee?" (25:44). The King will answer them, "Truly, I say to you, as you did it not to one of the least of these, you did it not to me" (25:45). The King also answers those whom He is welcoming to Heaven, "Truly, I say to you, as you did it to one of the least of these my brethren, you did it to me" (25:40). Mother Teresa emphasized that Jesus did not say, "You did it for me"; Jesus said, "You did it to me."[5]

Venerable Aloysius Schwartz, known as "Fr. Al" to the Sisters of Mary whom he founded, and the children in the many World Villages for Children he established, takes this a step further, calling this the "Sacrament of Poverty":

> Christ's presence in the poor marvelously complements his presence in the Eucharist. In the Sacrament of the Eucharist, the Son of God gives himself to us in the form of bread, and we approach the table of communion as spiritual beggars with outstretched hand and hungry heart. In "the sacrament of poverty" the roles are mysteriously reversed. Christ is now the beggar, and he humbly approaches us and pleads for bread.[6]

When we consecrate ourselves to the Holy Family, we are uniting our lives to Jesus, living with our brother as He walks to the Cross. We are embracing, in obedience, the poverty of the Holy Family as well as the beauty.

Pray the Litany of the Holy Family *(page 207).*

DAY 30

Holy Family, poor in material goods, but rich in divine blessings, have pity on us

> And when the time came for their purification according to the law of Moses, they brought him up to Jerusalem to present him to the Lord (as it is written in the law of the Lord, "Every male that opens the womb shall be called holy to the Lord") and to offer a sacrifice according to what is said in the law of the Lord, "a pair of turtledoves, or two young pigeons."
>
> — Lk 2:22–24

The Holy Family made an offering of two doves because they could not afford to offer a lamb. There is something stirring in this: The Family of the Lamb of God could not afford to offer a lamb to God. This passage suggests that Mary and Joseph were poor, but also uniquely rich among all those bound to the Law. The Holy Family offers these sacrifices at the Temple, these good works, though unnecessary, out of the abundance of their divine blessings. According to the Law of Moses, a mother was required to undergo ritual purification after giving birth to be "[cleansed] from the flow of her blood" (Lev 12:7). Yet Mary's pregnancy was unique among all pregnancies, and the flow of Blood from her Baby, the Lamb of God, would one day cleanse all mankind. In the purification rite, the priest offered a lamb or two doves to "make atonement for her" (Lev 12:7). And yet, Mary will one day stand at the foot of the Cross and offer her Son to God in atonement for the sins of all mankind. The two doves were offered by the priest, "one for a burnt offering and the other for a sin offering" (Lev 12:8). And yet, Mary was sinless and had no need of purification. In the end, we see from the Holy Family's offerings, not their material poverty, but their incredible riches. This same family welcomes you as one of their own. It's a tremendous invitation, but you won't recognize its immensity if you look upon the Holy Family merely as the world sees them.

The Divinity of Jesus

> He who makes rich is made poor; He takes on the poverty of my flesh, that I may gain the riches of his divinity.[1]
>
> — St. Gregory Nazianzen

Jesus could have been born into any family, but He chose this Family. He could have been born as the Son of the Roman Emperor. He could have chosen any of the richest and most powerful families on earth, but instead He chose the family of a carpenter in Nazareth. From the outside looking in, it's a strange choice, even a scandalous one, like the scandal of the Cross. The early Christian apologists were forced to answer for the poverty and death of Jesus. Here is St. Augustine's answer to the paradox of poverty:

> He who is the Bread of Life hungered; He who is the Fountain thirsted; He who is the Light slept; He who is the Way was wearied by the journey; He who is the Truth was accused by false witnesses; He who is the Judge of the living and the dead was judged by a mortal judge; He who is Justice was condemned by the unjust; He who is the Teacher of all was beaten with whips; He who is the Vine was crowned with thorns; He who is the Foundation was suspended upon a cross; He who is Strength was weakened; He who is Health was wounded; He who is Life died.[2]

The answer then was as simple as it is today. Jesus did choose the richest family on earth — "rich" as seen through God's eyes, not the world's. He chose a family for us, and He chose well. Jesus brought together the greatest man and the greatest woman on earth to be the greatest father and mother in history for us.

God's greatest blessing to the Holy Family was, of course, Himself. Jesus is the treasure of all treasures. He is not only the giver and source of all riches but the ultimate object of all our desires, the end of all our longings. We shouldn't ask to possess riches; instead we should ask to be His possession, to be possessed by God. These riches are described by St. John of the Cross: "Christ is like a rich mine with many pockets containing treasures: however deep we dig we will never find their end or their limit. Indeed, in every pocket new seams of fresh riches are discovered on all sides."[3] Jesus is the treasure from which all treasures flow.

The Sinlessness of Mary

> At Lourdes, the Immaculata did not say of herself that she had been conceived immaculately, but, as St. Bernadette repeated, *Que soy era immaculada councepciou*: "I am the Immaculate Conception." If among human beings the wife takes the name of her husband because she belongs to him, is one with him, is equal to him and is, with him, the source of new life, with how much greater reason should the name of the Holy Spirit, who is the divine Immaculate Conception, be used as the name of her in whom he lives as uncreated Love, the principle of life in the whole supernatural order of grace?[4]
>
> — St. Maximilian Kolbe

The great mercy that is Mary's Immaculate Conception has never been equaled in human history. It stands alone. All the gold in the world pales in comparison. And yet, Mary's sinlessness is only the fruit of something deeper and richer, namely, the mercy of God. In this sense, compared to all other humans, Mary's relationship with the Trinity is unique. She is the daughter of the Father, the mother of the Son, and the spouse of the Holy Spirit.

The angel Gabriel — who transmitted the marriage proposal from God Himself — told Mary how her espousal to the Holy Spirit and divine motherhood would happen. The two are intrinsically linked: "The Holy Spirit will come upon you, and the power of the Most High will overshadow you; therefore the child to be born will be called holy, the Son of God" (Lk 1:35). Therefore, as St. Maximilian Kolbe tells us above, Mary was not merely immaculately conceived. Mary *is* the Immaculate Conception. She is the spouse of the Holy Spirit, who is the uncreated Immaculate Conception. At the Annunciation, Mary receives a new married name from her spouse. She receives her earthly married name from Joseph, who also names Jesus, by the way; and she receives her heavenly married name from the Holy Spirit. This is why Mary gives St. Bernadette her heavenly name when appearing from Heaven.

This is another reason why becoming members of the Holy Family also makes us members of God's family. We become God's own family, not just through Jesus, but through Mary, too. How do we gain the immeasurable riches of the Holy Spirit and the unfathomable riches of Jesus? How do we plumb the depths of these riches? Saint Louis de Montfort provides the answer in *True Devotion to the Blessed Virgin*: "Mary is the safest, easiest, shortest and most perfect way of approaching Jesus."[5] The splintering of Protestantism into thousands of different sects and denominations shows us that Christians can often become confused and scattered in their pursuit of Christ and fall into error. Ironically, many of these sects are founded on "going straight to Jesus," and yet lead the faithful astray. Paradoxically, devotion to Mary is the best way to go straight to Jesus.

Why? Because the mother keeps the family together. And Mary is no ordinary mother. Her motherhood is divine because her motherhood is directly endowed by God the Father, directly actualized by the God the Holy Spirit, and the direct fruit of her motherhood is God the Son. Mary's sinlessness is one of the greatest treasures in human history, if not the greatest. Yet it's just one facet of who Mary is. It points to something about her nature as the Immaculate Conception and her role as the new Mother of the whole human race. We are united to Jesus through Mary. Because she was never led astray by sin, she will keep us on the right path. Just as Mary, unhindered by sin, always kept her gaze fixed on Jesus, she will keep us fixed on her Son. This is not just a Catholic idea; it's a fundamental element of God's plan for our salvation. As Jesus came to us through Mary, it's through Mary that we should go to Him.[6] It's rightly said, "For there is one God, and there is one mediator between God and men, the man Christ Jesus" (1 Tim 2:5). There is one mediator between God and man — Jesus, the hypostatic union of God and man — but who should mediate between Jesus and man? The answer is anyone. Every single one of us may mediate between our brothers and Jesus by praying for each other. There is one mediator, however, who rises above all of us. This is Jesus' own Mother, the New Queen-Mother of Israel, the Queen of Heaven. She is the most beautiful of all Jesus' treasures. St. John Eudes wrote, "The Heart of Mary is a treasure of holiness and love, the source of all virtues, and the refuge of sinners."[7]

The Greatness of St. Joseph

> If you wish to be close to Christ, we again today repeat, "Go to Joseph!" ("*Ite ad Ioseph!*")[8]
>
> — Venerable Pope Pius XII

> Go to Joseph ("*Ite ad Ioseph!*") and do whatever he tells you!
>
> — Gen 41:55

> He made him lord of his house and ruler of all his possessions.
>
> — Ps 105:21

Saint Joseph bore the name of Joseph, the son of Jacob. Jacob and Joseph were two of the greatest patriarchs of the Old Testament. This is very significant. The pharaoh of Egypt adopted Joseph into his own family, so that he was regarded as a son of Pharaoh. Joseph was given great authority. Pharaoh "made him lord of his house and ruler of all his possessions" (Ps 105:21). Joseph was placed in charge of all the granaries of Egypt. At that time, Egypt was considered the world's breadbasket because it provided bread to all the world. Joseph correctly interprets Pharaoh's dreams, revealing that seven years of abundance of grain in Egypt would be followed by seven years of famine (Gen 41:28–32). Joseph, being a wise servant, prepared for the famine. He "stored up grain in great abundance, like the sand of the sea until he ceased to measure it, for it could not be measured" (Gen 41:49). When the famine struck, Pharaoh instructed all of Egypt: "Go to Joseph ("*Ite ad Ioseph!*") and what he says to you do" (Gen 41:55). Doctor of the Church St. Lawrence of Brindisi draws a parallel here between the actions of Joseph and St. Joseph: "Pharaoh, the mighty king of Egypt, exalted Joseph and made him the highest prince in his kingdom, because he stored up the grain and bread and saved the people of his entire kingdom. So Joseph saved and protected Christ, who is the living bread and gives eternal life to the world."[9]

Joseph of Egypt prefigured a much greater Joseph, St. Joseph, who would bring his Son, the Bread of Heaven, to safety in Egypt. Both Josephs safeguarded bread for the whole world, but St. Joseph protected, not food which perishes, but "the living bread which came down from Heaven; if any one eats of this bread, he will live for ever" (Jn 6:51). Pharaoh gave Joseph great authority, and God likewise made St. Joseph "lord of his house and ruler of all his possessions" (Ps 105:21). Saint Joseph was made lord of the house of Nazareth and ruler of all God's treasures, the greatest of these being Jesus and Mary. While the titles bestowed by Pharaoh were earthly and transitory in nature, the titles bestowed by God are eternal. Even now, St. Joseph is charged with guarding God's treasury of graces. Even now, we are to "Go to Joseph" ("*Ite ad Ioseph!*") and do whatever he tells us! (see also Gen 41:55).

Pray the Litany of the Holy Family (page 207).

DAY 31

Holy Family, as nothing in the eyes of men, but so great in Heaven, have pity on us

For he grew up before him like a young plant,
and like a root out of dry ground;
he had no form or comeliness that we should look at him,
and no beauty that we should desire him.
He was despised and rejected by men;
a man of sorrows, and acquainted with grief;
and as one from whom men hide their faces;
he was despised, and we esteemed him not.

— Is 53:2–3

Isaiah prophesied that the Messiah would be unknown among men and common in appearance. His divinity would be hidden in the ordinary. Jesus would have an ordinary face, but it would be a face that would ravish hearts and scatter enemies. Psalm 68:1 says, "[L]et them that hate him flee from before his face" (Douay-Rheims Version, Ps 67:1 in this translation).[1] Jesus looked like an ordinary man, yet He has "the name above all names" (see also Phil 2:9). Saint Joseph appeared to be a common carpenter, but he was the hidden King of Israel and rightful heir to the throne of David. Mary looked like a common girl, but her Immaculate Conception had been prophesied since the beginning of time, and she was designed to be the New Eve, the mother of all the living, and the Queen of Heaven (see also Gen 3:15).

The Kingship of Jesus

The Solemnity of Our Lord Jesus Christ, King of the Universe, also known as Christ the King, is the last Sunday of the liturgical year. Pope Pius XI created this feast in 1925 to combat the rising tide of communism, atheism, and secularism. He further stated the liturgical feast's purpose, saying:

> It seems to Us that We cannot in a more fitting manner close this Holy Year, nor better signify Our gratitude and that of the whole of the Catholic world to Christ the immortal King of ages, for the blessings showered upon Us, upon the Church, and upon the Catholic world during this holy period … Nations will be reminded by the annual celebration of this feast that not only private individuals but also rulers and princes are bound to give public honor and obedience to Christ. It will call to their minds the thought of the last judgment, wherein Christ, who has been cast out of public life, despised, neglected and ignored, will most severely avenge these insults; for his kingly dignity demands that the State should take account of the commandments of God and of Christian principles, both in making laws and in administering justice, and also in providing for the young a sound moral education.[2]

What a powerful statement! Saint Cyril of Alexandria noted something similar, stating that Jesus "has dominion over all creatures, a dominion not seized by violence nor usurped, but his by essence and by nature."[3] Pope Leo XIII said that the empire of Jesus Christ, who is the Head and Supreme Lord of the human race, "includes not only Catholic nations, not only baptized persons who, though of right belonging to the Church, have been led astray by error, or have been cut off from her by schism, but also all those who are outside the Christian faith; so that truly the whole of mankind is subject to the power of Jesus Christ."[4] This is all according to the Great Commission given by Jesus' own words: "All authority in heaven and on earth has been given to me. Go therefore and make disciples of all nations, baptizing them in the name of the Father and of the Son and of the Holy Spirit, teaching them to observe all that I have commanded you; and lo, I am with you always, to the close of the age" (Mt 28:18–20).

The Lord Jesus Christ is given kingship, power, and authority over everything, and His royal charge to us is to baptize all nations. Baptism brings a person into the life of the earthly trinity, the Holy Family, and into the sublime reality of the Holy Trinity. By consecrating ourselves to the Holy Family, we are plunging into Jesus' royal mission as members of His royal family. Again, we see how our membership in the Holy Family will bring order to the world through the reign of Christ the King.

The Queenship of Mary

Thirty years after Pope Pius XI established the Solemnity of Christ the King in 1925, Venerable Pope Pius XII established the Feast of the Queenship of Mary and called for an annual renewal of the consecration of the human race to the Immaculate Heart of Mary, "cherishing the hope that through such consecration a new era may begin, joyous in Christian peace and in the triumph of religion."[5] Pope Pius XII explains in his encyclical *Ad Caeli Reginam* why it is fitting to call Our Lady "Queen of Heaven" and "Queen of the World":

> Now, in the accomplishing of this work of redemption, the Blessed Virgin Mary was most closely associated with Christ; and so it is fitting to sing in the sacred liturgy: "Near the cross of Our Lord Jesus Christ there stood, sorrowful, the Blessed Mary, Queen of Heaven and Queen of the World." Hence, as the devout disciple of St. Anselm wrote in the Middle Ages: "just as … God, by making all through his power, is Father and Lord of all, so the blessed Mary, by repairing all through her merits, is Mother and Queen of all; for God is the Lord of

> all things, because by His command He establishes each of them in its own nature, and Mary is the Queen of all things, because she restores each to its original dignity through the grace which she merited.[6]

God is "Father and Lord of all" because He created all, through the Son, by His own power. Mary is the "Mother and Queen of all" because she helps restore all of us to the original dignity of our creation through the grace which she merited from God. Grace sufficient for the whole human race flows through our Queen to us, as once the Lord of all came into the world through His virginal conception in her womb and virgin birth.

These singular, cosmic events occurred in the commonest of places, at least in the eyes of men: the Holy House of Nazareth and the stable of Bethlehem. Now, of course, great basilicas have been built in these common places, giving them the honor and sanctity they are due. This is because the Church, the worldwide Holy Family, makes visible the invisible greatness of Heaven.

The Lordship of St. Joseph

As Popes Pius XI and XII created feasts for the royal aspects of the Holy Family, Blessed Pope Pius IX honored the Lordship of St. Joseph. On the Feast of the Immaculate Conception, December 8, 1870, he declared St. Joseph the Patron of the Universal Church. He took this step because the venerable prelates of the whole Catholic world had petitioned him to do so. The leaders of the Church were begging for St. Joseph's help as they faced such troublesome times when "the Church [was] beset by enemies on every side, and [was] weighed down by calamities so heavy that ungodly men assert[ed] that the gates of hell have at length prevailed against [the Church.]"[7]

Pope Pius IX was not exaggerating. Armies of Masons were laying siege to the Vatican from the north and south, attempting to trample the Church into dust, not understanding the greatness of the Holy Family.

While shepherding the Church through a time of famine, pestilence, and war,[8] Pope Pius IX invoked St. Joseph, as prefigured by Joseph of Egypt, as was discussed yesterday:

> As almighty God appointed Joseph, son of the patriarch Jacob, over all the land of Egypt to save grain for the people, so when the fullness of time had come and He was about to send to earth His only-begotten Son, the Savior of the world, He chose another Joseph, of whom the first had been the type, and He made him the lord and chief of His household and possessions, the guardian of His choicest treasures. ... [Joseph] most diligently reared Him whom the faithful were to receive as the bread that came down from heaven whereby they might obtain eternal life.[9]

Saint Joseph's Lordship is also based on the fact that the King of the Cosmos was, in a real sense, subject to him: "Jesus Christ our Lord ... deigned to be reputed in the sight of men as the son of Joseph, and was subject to him."[10] There, in the humble home of Nazareth, without guard or grand entrance, "Him whom countless kings and prophets had desired to see, Joseph not only saw but conversed with, and embraced in paternal affection, and kissed."[11]

The source of eternal life, which explorers would circumnavigate the globe in search of, the locus of all future pilgrimages, was unvisited, unsought, and unknown in the home of Joseph. "Those who are of noble birth," like St. Joseph, "may learn, from this Family of royal blood, how to live simply in times of prosperity, and how to retain their dignity in times of distress."[12]

We consecrate ourselves to the Holy Family in order that we may be consecrated to the three Hearts of the Holy House of Nazareth: the Sacred Heart, the Immaculate Heart, and the Most Chaste Heart. Because of the sublime dignity which God conferred on His most faithful servant, we ask that St. Joseph would intercede for us, too, in times of trouble.

Pray the Litany of the Holy Family (page 207).

DAY 32

Holy Family, our support in life and our hope in death, have pity on us

> How easy it is to die with Jesus on the cross — if one has lived with Jesus on the cross![1]
>
> — St. Alphonsus Liguori

The Holy Family helps us enter more intimately into the life of Jesus, which conquers the power of sin and death in our lives. The Holy House of Nazareth, as Pope St. Paul VI states, is the "school where we begin to understand the life of Jesus — the school of the Gospel."[2] In our time in this humble home, we learn "the importance of family life, its communion of love, its austere and simple beauty, and its sacred and inviolable character."[3] The Holy Family was destined by God to be the pattern for all other families. Nazareth is also the school of virtue, where we learn to grow in faith despite the trials of life. Pope Leo XIII taught that the Holy Family "displayed every virtue which can be called forth by an ordinary home life, with its mutual services of charity … and its practices of godly piety."[4]

In our families, our hopes and dreams in life come to fruition. In the family, we also learn about the harsh and painful reality of death. We all remember the first time one of our family members died, whether in our immediate or distant family. The Holy Family teaches us to have hope when a death occurs in the family. Just as they teach us to live with Christ, they help us to rise with Him as well. As we pray in the "Hail, Holy Queen," if we live with the Holy Family, Mary will serve as our "Most Gracious Advocate" in our hour before the judgment seat, and as St. Joseph protected the Holy Family on their journeys, he will protect us, too, on our final pilgrimage to Heaven.

Live and Die for Jesus!

> Hold the cross high so I may see it through the flames.[5]
>
> — St. Joan of Arc

These words were Joan of Arc's last testament while she was being burned at the stake on May 30, 1431. Similarly, before being devoured by wild beasts under Emperor Trajan in A.D. 107, St. Ignatius of Antioch wrote, "I would prefer to die in Jesus Christ than to rule over all the earth."[6] Before being beheaded by the orders of King Henry VIII on July 6, 1535, St. Thomas More told those assembled, "I die the King's good servant, and God's first."[7] If we live with Christ, we will have the courage to die with Him as well, as the great martyrs did. We will learn to keep our eyes fixed on Jesus, as St. Joan of Arc did; to prefer Jesus to riches and power, as St. Ignatius of Antioch did; and to be a good servant of Christ, as St. Thomas More was. These are the lessons of Nazareth and the gifts of the Holy Family.

The Holy House of Nazareth is the home of martyrs and the school of martyrdom. "The Passion of Jesus," St. Bernard of Clairvaux says, "began with his birth."[8] The Holy Family walked the road to Calvary, the *Via Dolorosa*, together. Saint Joseph guarded and protected the Holy Family for as many days as God gave him, all the while knowing that God would not allow him to be there at the end. As the great protector of Jesus and Mary, Joseph's living martyrdom was particularly acute.

This is especially true of the Blessed Mother. As St. Alphonsus teaches us, "Mary is the Queen of Martyrs, for her Martyrdom was longer and greater than that of all the Martyrs."[9] An angel revealed to St. Bridget, "that the Blessed Virgin, even before she became [Christ's] mother, knowing how much the Incarnate Word was to suffer for the salvation of men, and [suffering with] this innocent Saviour, who was to be so cruelly put to death for crimes not his own, even then began her great martyrdom."[10] Jesus is called the King of Sorrows and the King of Martyrs because "he suffered during his life more than all other martyrs." Similarly, Mary is the Queen of Martyrs and the Mother of Sorrows, "having merited this title by suffering the most cruel martyrdom possible after that of her son."[11]

Think of Jesus growing up in the company of these saints who were the greatest of all. These spiritual parents to the martyrs were His parents. When we consecrate ourselves to the Holy Family, we enter under the roof of Nazareth and, along with all the martyrs, live in the shadow of Calvary.

Mary: Our Life, Our Sweetness, and Our Hope

Hail, Holy Queen, Mother of Mercy,
our life, our sweetness, and our hope.
To thee do we cry,
poor banished children of Eve.
To thee do we send up our sighs,
mourning and weeping in this valley of tears.
Turn then, most gracious advocate,
thine eyes of mercy toward us,
and after this our exile,
show unto us the blessed fruit of thy womb, Jesus.
O clement, O loving, O sweet Virgin Mary.

V. Pray for us, O holy Mother of God.

R. That we may be made worthy of the promises of Christ.

Prayerfully consider the words of the *Salve Regina* given above. In both the *Salve Regina* and the *Ave Maria*, we're invoking Mary's help at the hour of our death: "Holy Mary, Mother of God, pray for us sinners, now and at the hour of our death." In the *Salve Regina*, we pray, "Turn then, most gracious advocate, thine eyes of mercy toward us." These aren't just artful phrases, repeated across the centuries merely for repetition's sake. They're not empty words, but powerful pleas for the assistance of Our Lady.

At the hour of our death, just nanoseconds after our life ends, we'll be standing before Jesus. This is called the Particular Judgment. Those who die before the Second Coming will be judged immediately at their deaths, as we read in the Letter to the Hebrews, "It is appointed to men to die once, and after that comes the judgment" (9:27). At the Particular Judgment, we will receive reward or punishment based on our deeds in life: "[E]ach shall receive his wages, according to his labor" (1 Cor 3:8).

It's at this moment that the Blessed Mother can intercede for us as our "Most Gracious Advocate." Father Steven Scheier underwent his Particular Judgment as part of his near-death experience. Though he had planned to have his excuses ready, there was "no time."[12] He heard Jesus say that his "sentence is hell," but that's not all he heard:

> Then I heard a female voice [say], "Son, will you please spare his life and his eternal soul?" He said, "Mother, he's been a priest for twelve years for himself and not for me. Let him reap the punishment he deserves." She continued by saying, "But Son, we can give him special graces and strengths and then see if there's fruit. If not, your will be done." There is a very short pause. [Jesus came] back. He said, "Mother, he's yours." Ever since then, I have been hers.[13]

Not all of us get a second chance in death, but, if you are reading this, your second chance is now. Begin your consecration to the Holy Family with Confession if needed. This is why we consecrate ourselves to the Holy Family. One day our hour will come, and we'll all have to face the Particular Judgment.

But we don't have to face it alone. This is why we invoke Mary as our "Holy Queen, [our] Mother of Mercy, our life, our sweetness, and our hope." She is our hope at the hour of our death. She is the Queen-Mother who intercedes for us before the King and begs for His mercy for us. Pray now that she will always be at your side and that of your loved ones.

St. Joseph: Patron of a Happy Death

> When Joseph was dying, Mary sat at the head of his bed, holding him in her arms. Jesus stood just below her near Joseph's breast. The whole room was brilliant with light and full of angels. After his death, his hands were crossed on his breast, he was wrapped from head to foot in a white winding sheet, laid in a narrow casket, and placed in a very beautiful tomb, the gift of a good man. Only a few men followed the coffin with Jesus and Mary; but I saw it accompanied by angels and environed with light. Joseph's remains were afterward removed by the Christians to Bethlehem, and interred. I think I can still see him lying there incorrupt.[14]
>
> — Blessed Anne Catherine Emmerich

This is why St. Joseph is called the "Patron of a Happy Death." He was loathe to leave his family without protection from the torments that lay ahead for them; and yet, at the moment of his death, Jesus and Mary were at his bedside, holding him in their arms. This is the kind of death we all long for: being welcomed into Heaven in a room brilliant with light and full of angels, carried there in the arms of Jesus and Mary. Saint Joseph was the first to die thus, the first of many. We pray that if we live with the Holy Family, we may also die in their arms.

Joseph and Mary work together at the hour of our death. While Mary is our "most gracious advocate," St. Joseph is our guardian in death. According to St. Alphonsus Liguori, "At that moment [of death] especially the devil puts forth all his power to gain the soul that is passing into eternity; knowing that the time is short in which he may win her, and that if he loses her, he has lost her forever."[15] The devil makes one last attempt for our souls at the moment of our death, and he tries all the harder knowing that he may be about to lose a soul eternally. But we need not fear if we are guarded and concealed from Satan by St. Joseph, Terror of Demons. Saint Joseph, who once concealed the Virgin Birth from the devil, will conceal us beneath his cloak, as he concealed the Holy Family during their flight into Egypt; and on our flight from this life into the next, when we are beset by Satan's legions, St. Joseph will conceal us within the folds of his cloak, as once he concealed the Holy Family from Herod's armies.

> It is, then, natural and worthy that as the Blessed Joseph ministered to all the needs of the family at Nazareth and girt it about with his protection, he should now cover with the cloak of his heavenly patronage and defend the Church of Jesus Christ.[16]
>
> — Pope Leo XIII

Pray the Litany of the Holy Family (page 207).

DAY 33

Consecration Day

O God of goodness and mercy, grant that we may always honour and imitate Jesus, Mary, and Joseph; so that, pleasing them on earth, we may enjoy their presence in heaven; through the same Jesus Christ Our Lord. Amen[1]

You've made it!

Today, you're going to consecrate yourself to the Holy Family. A program of consecration to the Holy Family has been long in the making. This consecration to the Holy Family has many forebears, but certainly St. José Manyanet is among them. He's the "Apostle of the Holy Family" and the priest who was instrumental in Pope Leo XIII's establishment of the Feast of the Holy Family, which is always celebrated on the Sunday after Christmas Day.[2] This consecration to the Holy Family is the root and foundation of the 33 Day Consecrations to the Blessed Virgin Mary and St. Joseph.

Love the Holy Family

Blessed Holy Family,
Blessed are you a thousand times over,
For with your glory you recreate
The infinite Majesty.
To you, exquisite beauty,
Weeping for my mistakes
And past deviations,
I surrender my heart.
Look upon me with compassion!
Do not abandon me, my Parents!!![3]

— St. José Manyanet

Surrender your heart to the Holy Family, as St. José Manyanet prays above. It should be easy to love them, who teach us the meaning of love. With great joy, enter the Nazarene (which means "consecration") home of the Holy Family. Put before your eyes the great ones whom you should love on earth — Jesus, Mary, and Joseph. Here you will find the love for which you were made and the death for which we are all striving, a holy and happy one. And in this death, you will find Jesus, Mary, and Joseph.

Every saint has lived in the humble home of Nazareth, in the Hearts of Jesus, Mary, and Joseph, and each saint has died with them, too. All the saints are now reunited with Jesus, Mary, and Joseph in Heaven. Don't you want to be in that number? Don't you want to see the Holy Family in Heaven? Every saint has sought to honor and love the Holy Family with filial devotion and obedience. You will now be among those who have entered the Holy House of Nazareth through consecration to them.

Welcome to the Holy Family!

Defend the Holy Family

We have discussed in-depth how the Holy Family will defend us in life and death. But it's also important for *us* to defend the Holy Family. Once we have fallen in love with them and began to reflect their virtues and values, it's important that we defend the family as an institution modeled on the Holy Family. Pope St. John Paul II, who witnessed firsthand the destruction of society that arises from attacks on the family, instructs us on this defense:

> At the school of Nazareth, every family learns to be a workshop of love, unity, and openness to life. In our day a misunderstood sense of rights sometimes troubles the very nature of the family institution and of the conjugal bond. People who believe in *the importance of the family based on marriage* should join forces at all levels. The family is a human and divine reality that should be defended and promoted as a fundamental social good.[4]

As Pope St. John Paul II describes above, we are witnessing a deformation of the family based on the malformation of human rights. The freedom of bodily autonomy, for example, doesn't include the right to kill an unborn child. The freedom to marry doesn't grant us the right to restructure marriage and even gender. So many evils seem to plague society and the family at this moment in history that it can seem overwhelming. Don't fear. Raise the banner of the Holy Family. They will lead us to solutions. Defend and promote the Holy Family.

Promote the Holy Family

> [Eve] was that vineyard whose enclosure her own hands had enabled death to violate, so that she could taste its fruit; thus the mother of all the living became the source of death for every living creature. But in her stead Mary grew up, a new vine in place of the old. Christ, the new life, dwelt within her ... He who was also the carpenter's glorious son set up his cross above death's all-consuming jaws, and led the human race into the dwelling place of life. Since a tree had brought about the downfall of mankind, it was upon a tree that mankind crossed over to the realm of life. Bitter was the branch that had once been grafted upon that ancient tree, but sweet the young shoot that has now been grafted in, the shoot in which we are meant to recognize the Lord whom no creature can resist.[5]
>
> — St. Ephrem the Syrian

The Holy Family is the Holy Family Tree, the New Tree of Life. Jesus is the "young shoot ... grafted in," the "righteous branch," that grew from the family tree of David, the "stump of Jesse" that arose through Joseph, the carpenter, whose Son was hammered to the Cross. Jesus is also the "true vine," which sprang from Mary, "the new vine" of Eve, as described above. How do you promote the growth of a tree or vine or any living thing? Help it grow. Be a new branch of the Holy Family, a new shoot. Through the Sacraments of the Church we, too, are grafted onto this Holy Family Tree. Grow and encourage others to grow as part of this family.

The Holy Trinity wants the Holy Family to be better known and loved. God wants the Holy Family to be enshrined in every home so that every home may become a part of the Holy House of Nazareth. As Pope St. John Paul II enjoined us above, "The family is a human and divine reality that should be defended and promoted as a fundamental social good."[6] We defend and promote the family by defending and promoting the Holy Family.

The best way to promote the Holy Family is to become a part of its beauty, a great branch of that beautiful family tree. "May Nazareth (place of the 'branch') teach us what family life is, its communion of love, its austere and simple beauty, and its sacred and inviolable character."[7] Grow so close to the Holy Family that you can ask them how you can promote them and this consecration. To commemorate the day of your consecration, you may want to enthrone an image of the Holy Family in your home. Timing your consecration (or your parish-wide consecration) so that it finishes on the Feast of the Holy Family would be a beautiful way to celebrate that Feast as well.

Never forget what you have learned in these days preparing for your consecration to the Holy Family. Renew your consecration frequently, even daily, by reciting the Act of Consecration to the Holy Family. Strive to please the Hearts of the Holy Family: the Sacred Heart, the Immaculate Heart, and the Most Chaste Heart. Enthrone these Hearts in your home. Graft yourself onto the sacramental life of this tree. Avoid sin, so as not to be cut off from the life of this tree, and live as a faithful member of the Church, which is the Holy Family brought to the world. Should scandals persist in the Church and society, keep your eyes fixed on Jesus, Mary, and Joseph. They will never disappoint you. They will never abandon you. They will always love you and be with you.

> [C]ontemplate the *Holy Family of Nazareth*, a wonderful model of human and supernatural virtues for all Christian families. Let us meditate on the mystery of this unique family: we can find in it values and teachings which today are more indispensable than ever to give human society sound and stable foundations.[8]

— Pope St. John Paul II

> When God in his mercy determined to accomplish the work of man's renewal, which same had so many long ages awaited, he appointed and ordained this work on such wise that its very beginning might shew to the world the august spectacle of a Family which was known to be divinely constituted; that therein all men might behold a perfect model, as well of domestic life as of every virtue and pattern of holiness: for such indeed was the Holy Family of Nazareth.[9]

— Pope Leo XIII

Pray the Litany of the Holy Family (page 207).

Pray the Act of Consecration to the Holy Family (page 217).

PRAYERS

Litany of the Holy Family

Lord, have mercy. *Lord, have mercy.*
Christ, have mercy. *Christ, have mercy.*
Lord, have mercy. *Lord, have mercy.*

God, the Father of Heaven, *have mercy on us.*
God the Son, Redeemer of the World, *have mercy on us.*
God, the Holy Spirit, *have mercy on us.*
Holy Trinity, One God, *have mercy on us.*

Jesus, Mary, and Joseph, *have pity on us.*
Jesus, Mary, and Joseph, most worthy of our veneration, *have pity on us.*
Jesus, Mary, and Joseph, called "The Holy Family" from all time, *have pity on us.*
Jesus, Mary, and Joseph, Son, Mother, and Father of the Holy Family, *have pity on us.*
Jesus, Mary, and Joseph, Divine Child, pure spouse, and chaste spouse, *have pity on us*
Jesus, Mary, and Joseph, Restorers of fallen families, *have pity on us.*
Jesus, Mary, and Joseph, Image of the Blessed Trinity here on earth, *have pity on us.*

Holy Family, tested by the greatest of difficulties, *have pity on us.*
Holy Family, with much suffering on the journey to Bethlehem, *have pity on us.*
Holy Family, without a welcome in Bethlehem, *have pity on us.*
Holy Family, visited by the poor shepherds, *have pity on us.*
Holy Family, obliged to live in a stable, *have pity on us.*
Holy Family, praised by the angels, *have pity on us.*
Holy Family, venerated by the Wise Men from the East, *have pity on us.*
Holy Family, greeted by the pious Simeon in the Temple, *have pity on us.*

Holy Family, persecuted and exiled
to a foreign country, *have pity on us.*
Holy Family, hidden and unknown
in Nazareth, *have pity on us.*
Holy Family, faithful in observance
of divine laws, *have pity on us.*
Holy Family, perfect model of the
Christian family, *have pity on us.*
Holy Family, center of peace and
concord, *have pity on us.*
Holy Family, whose protector is a model
of paternal care, *have pity on us.*
Holy Family, whose mother is a model
of maternal diligence, *have pity on us.*
Holy Family, whose Divine Child is a
model of filial obedience, *have pity on us.*
Holy Family, poor in material goods,
but rich in divine blessings, *have pity on us.*
Holy Family, as nothing in the eyes of
men, but so great in Heaven, *have pity on us.*
Holy Family, our support in life and
our hope in death, *have pity on us.*

Lamb of God, who take away the sins of the world,
spare us, O Lord

Lamb of God, who take away the sins of the world,
hear us, O Lord

Lamb of God, who take away the sins of the world,
have mercy on us

Let us pray:

O God of infinite goodness and kindness, who has seen fit to call us to this family, give us the grace to venerate Jesus, Mary, and Joseph so that, imitating them in this life, we may enjoy with them the life to come. We ask this through Jesus Christ, our Lord. Amen.

Litany of the Holy Spouses

Lord, have mercy. *Lord, have mercy.*
Christ, have mercy. *Christ, have mercy.*
Lord, have mercy. *Lord, have mercy.*

God our Father in Heaven, *have mercy on us.*
God the Son, Redeemer of the world, *have mercy on us.*
God the Holy Spirit, *have mercy on us.*
Holy Trinity, one God, *have mercy on us.*

Holy Mary, *pray for us.*
Saint Joseph, *pray for us.*
Holy Spouses, *pray for us.*
Holy parents of Jesus, *pray for us.*
Holy protectors of the Body of Christ, *pray for us.*
Teachers of the Holy Child, *pray for us.*
Holy Virgins, *pray for us.*
Spouses most loving, *pray for us.*
Spouses most faithful, *pray for us.*
Spouses most pure, *pray for us.*
Spouses most just, *pray for us.*
Spouses most obedient, *pray for us.*
Spouses most humble, *pray for us.*
Spouses most generous, *pray for us.*
Models of family life, *pray for us.*
Models for couples, *pray for us.*
Models of parenthood, *pray for us.*
Parents to those without parents, *pray for us.*
Patrons of the unborn, *pray for us.*
Models for virgins, *pray for us.*
Lovers of poverty, *pray for us.*
Comfort of the troubled, *pray for us.*
Patrons of emigrants, *pray for us.*
Servants of the Lord, *pray for us.*
Ministers of Salvation, *pray for us.*
Mother and Patron of the Church, *pray for us.*

Lamb of God, Who take away the sins of the world,
spare us, O Lord.

Lamb of God, Who take away the sins of the world,
hear us, O Lord.

Lamb of God, Who take away the sins of the world,
have mercy on us.

V. The Virgin Mary was betrothed to Joseph of the house of David.

R. *Jesus was obedient to them and grew in wisdom, stature, and grace.*

Let us pray:

Holy Father, who joined together by a virginal bond the glorious Mother of your Son and the just man, Saint Joseph, that they might be faithful cooperators in the mystery of the Word Incarnate, we beseech you, that by meditating upon the mysteries of the Incarnation, hidden life, ministry, Passion, death, and Resurrection of your only begotten Son, we may live in more intimate union with Christ and may walk more joyfully in the way of love, through the same Christ our Lord. Amen.[1]

Litany of the Sacred Heart of Jesus

Lord, have mercy. *Lord, have mercy.*
Christ, have mercy. *Christ, have mercy.*
Lord, have mercy. *Lord, have mercy.*

Christ, hear us. *Christ, hear us.*
Christ, graciously hear us. *Christ, graciously hear us.*

God, the Father of Heaven, *have mercy on us.*
God the Son, Redeemer of the world, *have mercy on us.*
God the Holy Spirit, *have mercy on us.*
Holy Trinity, One God, *have mercy on us.*

Heart of Jesus, Son of the Eternal Father, *have mercy on us.*
Heart of Jesus, formed by the Holy Spirit in the womb of the Virgin Mother, *have mercy on us.*
Heart of Jesus, substantially united to the Word of God, *have mercy on us.*
Heart of Jesus, of Infinite Majesty, *have mercy on us.*
Heart of Jesus, Sacred Temple of God, *have mercy on us.*
Heart of Jesus, Tabernacle of the Most High, *have mercy on us.*
Heart of Jesus, House of God and Gate of Heaven, *have mercy on us.*
Heart of Jesus, burning furnace of charity, *have mercy on us.*
Heart of Jesus, abode of justice and love, *have mercy on us.*
Heart of Jesus, full of goodness and love, *have mercy on us.*
Heart of Jesus, abyss of all virtues, *have mercy on us.*
Heart of Jesus, most worthy of all praise, *have mercy on us.*
Heart of Jesus, King and center of all hearts, *have mercy on us.*
Heart of Jesus, in whom are all treasures of wisdom and knowledge, *have mercy on us.*
Heart of Jesus, in whom dwells the fullness of Divinity, *have mercy on us.*
Heart of Jesus, in whom the Father was well pleased, *have mercy on us.*
Heart of Jesus, of whose fullness we have all received, *have mercy on us.*
Heart of Jesus, desire of the everlasting hills, *have mercy on us.*
Heart of Jesus, patient and most merciful, *have mercy on us.*
Heart of Jesus, enriching all who invoke Thee, *have mercy on us.*
Heart of Jesus, fountain of life and holiness, *have mercy on us.*
Heart of Jesus, propitiation for our sins, *have mercy on us.*
Heart of Jesus, loaded down with opprobrium, *have mercy on us.*
Heart of Jesus, bruised for our offenses, *have mercy on us.*

Heart of Jesus, obedient to death, *have mercy on us.*
Heart of Jesus, pierced with a lance, *have mercy on us.*
Heart of Jesus, source of all consolation, *have mercy on us.*
Heart of Jesus, our life and resurrection, *have mercy on us.*
Heart of Jesus, our peace and our reconciliation, *have mercy on us.*
Heart of Jesus, Victim for our sins *have mercy on us.*
Heart of Jesus, salvation of those who trust in Thee, *have mercy on us.*
Heart of Jesus, hope of those who die in Thee, *have mercy on us.*
Heart of Jesus, delight of all the saints, *have mercy on us.*

Lamb of God, Who take away the sins of the world, *spare us, O Lord.*

Lamb of God, Who take away the sins of the world, *hear us, O Lord.*

Lamb of God, Who take away the sins of the world, *have mercy on us.*

V. Jesus, meek and humble of heart.

R. *Make our hearts like unto Thine.*

Let us pray:

Almighty and eternal God, look upon the Heart of Thy most beloved Son and upon the praises and satisfaction which He offers Thee in the name of sinners; and to those who implore Thy mercy, in Thy great goodness, grant forgiveness in the name of the same Jesus Christ, Thy Son, who livest and reignest with Thee forever and ever. Amen.

Litany of Loreto

Lord, have mercy.	*Lord, have mercy.*
Christ, have mercy.	*Christ, have mercy.*
Lord, have mercy.	*Lord, have mercy.*
God, the Father of Heaven,	*have mercy on us.*
God the Son, Redeemer of the world,	*have mercy on us.*
God the Holy Spirit,	*have mercy on us.*
Holy Trinity, one God,	*have mercy on us.*
Holy Mary,	*pray for us.*
Holy Mother of God,	*pray for us.*
Holy Virgin of virgins,	*pray for us.*
Mother of Christ,	*pray for us.*
Mother of the Church,	*pray for us.*
Mother of Mercy,	*pray for us.*
Mother of divine grace,	*pray for us.*
Mother of Hope,	*pray for us.*
Mother most pure,	*pray for us.*
Mother most chaste,	*pray for us.*
Mother inviolate,	*pray for us.*
Mother undefiled,	*pray for us.*
Mother most amiable,	*pray for us.*
Mother admirable,	*pray for us.*
Mother of good counsel,	*pray for us.*
Mother of our Creator,	*pray for us.*
Mother of our Savior,	*pray for us.*
Virgin most prudent,	*pray for us.*
Virgin most venerable,	*pray for us.*
Virgin most renowned,	*pray for us.*
Virgin most powerful,	*pray for us.*
Virgin most merciful,	*pray for us.*
Virgin most faithful,	*pray for us.*
Mirror of justice,	*pray for us.*
Seat of Wisdom,	*pray for us.*
Cause of our joy,	*pray for us.*

Spiritual vessel, *pray for us.*
Vessel of honor, *pray for us.*
Singular vessel of devotion, *pray for us.*
Mystical rose, *pray for us.*
Tower of David, *pray for us.*
Tower of ivory, *pray for us.*
House of gold, *pray for us.*
Ark of the covenant, *pray for us.*
Gate of Heaven, *pray for us.*
Morning star, *pray for us.*
Health of the sick, *pray for us.*
Refuge of sinners, *pray for us.*
Solace of Migrants, *pray for us.*
Comfort of the afflicted, *pray for us.*
Help of Christians, *pray for us.*
Queen of Angels, *pray for us.*
Queen of Patriarchs, *pray for us.*
Queen of Prophets, *pray for us.*
Queen of Apostles, *pray for us.*
Queen of Martyrs, *pray for us.*
Queen of Confessors, *pray for us.*
Queen of Virgins, *pray for us.*
Queen of all Saints, *pray for us.*
Queen conceived without original sin, *pray for us.*
Queen assumed into Heaven, *pray for us.*
Queen of the most Holy Rosary, *pray for us.*
Queen of families, *pray for us.*
Queen of peace, *pray for us.*

V. Lamb of God, Who takes away the sins of the world,

R. *Spare us, O Lord.*

V. Lamb of God, Who takes away the sins of the world,

R. *Graciously hear us, O Lord.*

V. Lamb of God, Who takes away the sins of the world,

R. *Have mercy on us.*

V. Pray for us, O holy Mother of God.

R. *That we may be made worthy of the promises of Christ.*

Let us pray.

Grant, we beseech Thee, O Lord God, that we Thy servants may enjoy perpetual health of mind and body, and by the glorious intercession of blessed Mary, ever Virgin, may be freed from present sorrow and rejoice in eternal happiness. Through Christ our Lord. Amen.

Litany of St. Joseph

Lord, have mercy.	*Lord, have mercy.*
Christ, have mercy.	*Christ, have mercy.*
Lord, have mercy.	*Lord, have mercy.*
Christ, hear us.	*Christ, graciously hear us.*
God, the Father of Heaven,	*have mercy on us.*
God the Son, Redeemer of the world,	*have mercy on us.*
God the Holy Spirit,	*have mercy on us.*
Holy Trinity, One God,	*have mercy on us.*
Holy Mary,	*pray for us.*
Saint Joseph,	*pray for us.*
Noble Offspring of David,	*pray for us.*
Light of Patriarchs,	*pray for us.*
Spouse of the Mother of God,	*pray for us.*
Guardian of the Redeemer,	*pray for us.*
Chaste Guardian of the Virgin,	*pray for us.*
Foster-Father of the Son of God,	*pray for us.*
Zealous Defender of Christ,	*pray for us.*
Servant of Christ,	*pray for us.*

Minister of salvation, *pray for us.*
Head of the Holy Family, *pray for us.*

Joseph Most Just, *pray for us.*
Joseph Most Chaste, *pray for us.*
Joseph Most Prudent, *pray for us.*
Joseph Most Courageous, *pray for us.*
Joseph Most Obedient, *pray for us.*
Joseph Most Faithful, *pray for us.*

Mirror of Patience, *pray for us.*
Lover of Poverty, *pray for us.*
Model of Workmen, *pray for us.*
Glory of Domestic Life, *pray for us.*
Guardian of Virgins, *pray for us.*
Pillar of Families, *pray for us.*
Support in difficulties, *pray for us.*
Comfort of the Afflicted, *pray for us.*
Hope of the Sick, *pray for us.*
Patron of exiles, *pray for us.*
Patron of the afflicted, *pray for us.*
Patron of the poor, *pray for us.*
Patron of the Dying, *pray for us.*
Terror of Demons, *pray for us.*
Protector of the Holy Church, *pray for us.*

Lamb of God, Who takes away the sins of the world,
Spare us, O Lord.

Lamb of God, Who takes away the sins of the world,
Graciously hear us, O Lord.

Lamb of God, Who takes away the sins of the world,
Have mercy on us.

V. He has made him lord of his household,

R. *And prince over all his possessions.*

Let us pray.

O God, who, in your loving providence, chose Blessed Joseph to be the spouse of your most Holy Mother, grant us the favor of having him for our intercessor in Heaven whom on earth we venerate as our protector. You, who live and reign forever and ever. Amen.

Act of Consecration to the Holy Family

On this day, before the great multitude of heavenly witnesses, I, ________________, a repentant sinner, consecrate myself to the Holy Family. Jesus, Mary, and Joseph, I love you, now and for all eternity!

Lord Jesus, I give myself entirely to You. Your Sacred Heart, which burns with love for me, is my refuge and strength. May my heart always burn with love for You and be united with Your most holy will. Keep me always in Your Holy Family and Your Mystical Body, the Catholic Church, and never let me be separated from You. Through the aid of the Holy Spirit, help me to live a life of virtue, sacrifice, piety, holiness, and love. You are my all, and without You I am nothing. O Jesus, how I love You!

Mother Mary, I give myself entirely to you. You are my life, my sweetness, and my hope. Keep me always under your mantle and place me near your Immaculate Heart. With your help, I will pray the Rosary more fervently, receive Holy Communion more worthily, and go to Confession more often when needed. O sweetest Virgin, how I love you!

Saint Joseph, I give myself entirely to you. You are my spiritual father, and I am so grateful you are in my life. With Jesus and Mary, help me to live and die in a state of grace and enter into the presence of God the Father in Heaven. Keep me always under your paternal cloak and near your Most Chaste Heart. O Good St. Joseph, how I love you!

O Holy Family of Jesus, Mary, and Joseph, I consecrate myself to you forever! My past, present, and future are in your hands. I am full of confidence and trust, knowing that you love me and desire me to a member of your family. Thank you for the gift of knowing and loving you. Thank you for the invitation to be a member of your Holy Family. I am yours forever! Amen.

Daily Act of Consecration to the Holy Family

Jesus, Mary, and Joseph, I give myself entirely to you, and to show my devotion to you I consecrate to you this day my eyes, my ears, my mouth, my heart, my whole being without reserve. Wherefore, O Holy Family, since I am your own, keep me and guard me as your property and possession. Amen.

Act of Consecration of Christian Families to the Holy Family by St. José Manyanet

O Jesus, our most loving Redeemer, who, coming down from Heaven to enlighten the world with doctrine and example, desired to spend the greater part of your mortal life humble and submissive to Mary and Joseph in the humble dwelling of Nazareth, sanctifying that family, which was to be the model for all Christian families, graciously accept ours, which is now dedicated and consecrated to you. Protect it, guard it, and confirm in it your holy fear, the peace and concord of Christian charity, so that, conforming to the divine model of your Family, it may, without exception, attain eternal beatitude.

Mary, loving mother of Jesus and our mother, grant that Jesus, through your pious intercession, may accept this humble offering, and obtain for us his graces and blessings.

O Joseph, most holy guardian of Jesus and Mary, help us with your prayers in every temporal and spiritual need, so that, with Mary and you, we may eternally praise and bless our Divine Redeemer Jesus.[2]

Prayer to the Holy Family by St. José Manyanet

O most loving Jesus, who, with your ineffable virtues and the examples of your domestic life, sanctified the family you chose here on earth, look compassionately on ours, which, prostrate before you, calls upon you favorably. Remember that it is your family, because it is especially consecrated and dedicated to you.

Assist it graciously, defend it from all danger, help it in its needs, and give it the grace to persevere constantly in imitating your Holy Family, so that, faithfully serving and loving you during its mortal life, it may afterward eternally sing your praises in Heaven.

Mary, Most Sweet Mother, we turn to your intercession, certain that the Divine Son will hear your prayers.

And you too, O glorious Patriarch Saint Joseph, help us with your powerful patronage, and present to Jesus our vows through Mary's hands.

Jesus, Mary, and Joseph, enlighten us, help us, save us. Amen.[3]

Veni, Sancte Spiritus (Come, Holy Spirit)

Come, Holy Spirit,
send down those beams,
which sweetly flow in silent streams
from Thy bright throne above.

O come, Thou Father of the poor;
O come, Thou source of all our store,
come, fill our hearts with love.

O Thou, of comforters the best,
O Thou, the soul's delightful guest,
the pilgrim's sweet relief.

Rest art Thou in our toil, most sweet
refreshment in the noonday heat;
and solace in our grief.

O blessed Light of life Thou art;
fill with Thy light the inmost heart
of those who hope in Thee.

Without Thy Godhead nothing can,
have any price or worth in man,
nothing can harmless be.

Lord, wash our sinful stains away,
refresh from Heaven our barren clay,
our wounds and bruises heal.

To Thy sweet yoke our stiff necks bow,
warm with Thy fire our hearts of snow,
our wandering feet recall.

Grant to Thy faithful, dearest Lord,
whose only hope is Thy sure word,
the sevenfold gifts of grace.

Grant us in life Thy grace that we,
in peace may die and ever be,
in joy before Thy face.
Amen. Alleluia.

Endnotes

INTRODUCTION

[1] Pope Benedict XV, *Bonum Sane,* quoted in Francis L. Filas, SJ, *St. Joseph and Daily Christian Living* (Macmillan Co., 1959), 192.

DAY 1

[1] St. Charbel Makhlouf, quoted in Hanna Skandar, *Love is a Radiant Light: The Life and Words of St. Charbel,* trans. William J. Melcher (Angelico Press, 2014), 93–94.

[2] Sister Lucia dos Santos of Fatima, quoted in "Fatima Visionary Predicted 'Final Battle' Would Be Over Marriage, Family," Catholic News Agency, July 8, 2016.

[3] Pope John Paul II, *Gratissimam Sane* (Letter to Families), February 2, 1994, par. 5.

[4] Pope Paul VI, "Discourse to the *Equipes Notre Dame* Movement (May 4, 1970)," quoted in Pope John Paul II, Apostolic Exhortation *Redemptoris Custos,* par. 7.

[5] Pope Leo XIII, Apostolic Letter *Breve Neminem Fugit*, June 14, 1892.

[6] Skandar, *Love is a Radiant Light*, 93–94.

DAY 2

[1] Concluding Prayer of the Litany of the Holy Family, in Missionaries of the Holy Family, *Holy Family Prayer Book: Prayers for Every Family* (Liguori, 2012), 19.

[2] St. Philip Neri, quoted in Matthew Kelly, *The Wisdom of the Saints: 365 Days of Inspiration* (Blue Sparrow, 2022), 66.

[3] St. Bartolo Longo, *Il Mese di Marzo: In Onore di San Giuseppe,* 15th ed. (Pompei, Italy: Pontificio Santuario di Pompei, 2001), 87–88. Unpublished translation by Miss Ileana E. Salazar.

[4] See *Manual of the Archconfraternity of the Holy Family* (Quebec, 1875).

[5] See Missionaries of the Holy Family, *Holy Family Prayer Book: Prayers for Every Family.*

[6] Pope Leo XIII, Apostolic Letter *Breve Neminem Fugit*, June 14, 1892.

[7] St. Bernard of Clairvaux, quoted in Kelly, *The Wisdom of the Saints*, 48.

DAY 3

[1] Pope Leo XIII, encyclical *Immortale Dei*, 1885, par. 6.

[2] St. Ignatius of Loyola, *The Spiritual Exercises of St. Ignatius*, trans. Louis J. Puhl (Loyola University Press, 1951), 11.

[3] Pope Pius XII, encyclical *Mystici Corporis,* June 29, 1943, par. 30.

[4] Pope Pius XII, *Mystici Corporis*, par. 32, citing Eph 2:14–16.

DAY 4

[1] Pope Leo XIII, Apostolic Letter, *Breve Neminem Fugit*, June 14, 1892.

[2] Pope Paul VI, "An Address at the Basilica of the Annunciation in Nazareth" in *The Pope Speaks 9*, no. 1 (1964).

[3] Pope John Paul II, Angelus message, December 26, 2004.

[4] Ibid, see also *Gaudium et Spes*, n. 22.

[5] Pope John Paul II, Angelus message, December 30, 2001.

DAY 5

[1] St. Leo the Great (Christmas Homily), quoted in Pope Paul VI, encyclical *Marialis Cultus*, February 2, 1974, par. 19.

[2] Pope Paul VI, encyclical *Marialis Cultus*, February 2, 1974, par. 22.

[3] St. Bartolo Longo, quoted in Fr. Donald H. Calloway, MIC, *Consecration to St. Joseph: The Wonders of Our Spiritual Father* (Marian Press, 2020), 244.

[4] Pope Paul VI, *Marialis Cultus*, par. 26.

[5] St. Ildephonsus of Toledo, *De virginitate perpetua sanctae mariae*, Chapter XII: PL 96, 106.

[6] St. Maximilian Kolbe, in Fr. Marco Tasca, OFM, *The Writings of St. Maximilian Maria Kolbe,* vol. 1.

[7] Ibid.

DAY 6

[1] Pope John Paul II, "Homily at the Opening of the Third General Conference of the Latin American Episcopate," given at Puebla de Los Angeles, Mexico, January 28, 1979.

[2] Pope Benedict XVI, Angelus message, December 27, 2009.

[3] St. Catherine of Siena, *The Dialogue*, trans. Suzanne Noffke (New York: Paulist Press, 1980), 167; as cited in Liturgy of the Hours, April 29, St. Catherine's feast day.

[4] St. Anselm of Canterbury, *Monologion*, chap. 67 in *The Basic Writings: Proslogium, Monologium, Cur Deus Homo, and Gaunilo's In Behalf of the Fool*, trans. Sidney Norton Deane (Open Court Publishing, 1962), 87.

[5] St. Athanasius, *On the Incarnation*, trans. and ed. John Behr (St. Vladimir's Seminary Press, 2011), 93.

[6] *Catechism of the Catholic Church*, 2nd ed. (Vatican City: Libreria Editrice Vaticana, 2000), par. 460. Hereafter, *CCC*.

[7] St. Maximilian Kolbe, in Fr. Marco Tasca, OFM, *The Writings of St. Maximilian Maria Kolbe*, vol. 1.

[8] St. Francis de Sales, "An Act of Oblation to the Holy Trinity," in "Prayers to the Most Holy Trinity," iBreviary app.

[9] *CCC*, par. 460.

[10] Ibid.

DAY 8

[1] Pope Leo XIII, *Quamquam Pluries* (1889).

[2] St. Teresa of Ávila, *The Life of St. Teresa of Jesus, of the Order of Our Lady of Carmel*, chapter VI, par. 12.

[3] *Complete Works of St. José Manyanet*, vol. 4, ed. Josep M. Blanquet, SF, trans. Scott Smith, (Madrid: Biblioteca de Autores Cristianos, 2010), 285.

[4] For a list of the Corporal and Spiritual Works of Mercy, see *CCC* par. 2447: "The *works of mercy* are charitable actions by which we come to the aid of our neighbor in his spiritual and bodily necessities. Instructing, advising, consoling, comforting are spiritual works of mercy, as are forgiving and bearing wrongs patiently. The corporal works of mercy consist especially in feeding the hungry,

sheltering the homeless, clothing the naked, visiting the sick and imprisoned, and burying the dead."

[5] St. Thomas Aquinas, quoted in Fr. John A. Hardon, SJ, "Our Lady of Fatima in the Light of History," *Review for Religious* 6 (May 1947), 141.

[6] St. Alphonsus Liguori, *Glories of Mary* (Redemptorist Fathers, 1927), Part III, No. 5; Part V, No. 4.

[7] Ibid., see also Litany of St. Alphonsus Liguori: "Saint Alphonsus, preserved even till death from mortal sin, pray for us."

[8] Pope St. John XXIII, *Journal of a Soul*, trans. Dorothy White (Image Books, 1980), 425.

[9] The Holy See, *Directory on Popular Piety and the Liturgy*, Chapter VI. Veneration of the Saints and the Beatified, "St. Joseph," 218–223.

[10] Blessed Concepción Cabrera de Armida, *Pequeña Esmeralda* (Coyoacan, Mexico: Editorial La Cruz, 2021), 217. Unpublished translation by Miss Ileana E. Salazar.

DAY 9

[1] See also Jeremiah 33:26: "the seed of Abraham, Isaac, and Jacob."

[2] Pope Leo XIII, Apostolic Letter *Breve Neminem Fugit*, 1892.

[3] St. Thérèse of Lisieux, *St. Thérèse of Lisieux: Her Last Conversations*, trans. by John Clark, OCD (ICS Publications, 1975), 105. This quotation was from August 20, 1897 (just a month before she died).

[4] St. José Manyanet, *The Spirit of the Holy Family: A Collection of Spiritual Meditations*, 236.

DAY 10

[1] St. Peter Julian Eymard, *Month of St. Joseph* (Emmanuel Publications, 1948), 6–7.

[2] Pope Leo XIII, Apostolic Letter *Breve Neminem Fugit*, quoted in Francis L. Filas, SJ, *St. Joseph and Daily Christian Living* (Macmillan Co., 1959), 188.

[3] St. Thérèse of Lisieux, in Katie Yoder, "Mother's Day 2024: 12 Catholic Quotes on the Beauty of Motherhood," *Catholic News Agency*, May 12, 2024.

[4] Pope Pius XII, "Address to Midwives on the Nature of Their Profession," 1951.

[5] St. Teresa Benedicta of the Cross, *The Significance of Woman's Intrinsic Value in National Life* (1928) in *The Collected Works of Edith Stein: Essays on Woman*, trans. Freda Mary Oben (ICS Publications, 1987).

[6] Pope St. Pius X, *Quam Singulari*, "Decree of the Sacred Congregation of the Discipline of the Sacraments on First Communion," 1910.

[7] Pope John Paul II, quoted in Bill Donaghy, "The Art of Wonder," *Catholic Exchange*, August 1, 2006, https://catholicexchange.com/the-art-of-wonder/.

DAY 11

[1] Pope Pius XII, Encyclical *Sacra Virginitas*, March 25, 1954, par. 63–64, also citing Pope Leo XIII, encyclical *Mirae Caritatis*, 1902; A. L. XXII, 1902–1903.

[2] Committee to Protect Journalists, "Middle East Special Report: Picking Up the Pieces," *CPJ*, June 13, 2002, https://cpj.org/reports/2002/06/west-bank-june02.

[3] Alban Butler, *The Lives of the Fathers, Martyrs, and Other Principal Saints*, vol. 1 (Dublin: James Duffy, 1866), 589–590.

[4] St. Teresa Benedicta of the Cross, *The Collected Works of Edith Stein: Essays on Woman*, trans. Freda Mary Oben (ICS Publications, 1987), 4.

[5] Jacobus de Voragine, *The Golden Legend: Readings on the Saints*, trans. William Granger Ryan (Princeton University Press, 1993), 2:245–247.

[6] Mélanie Calvat described Our Lady of La Salette thus: "Her gaze was soft and penetrating. Her eyes seemed to speak to mine, but the conversation came from a profound and vivid feeling of love for the ravishing beauty which was liquefying me. The softness of her gaze, her air of incomprehensible kindness made me understand and feel that she was drawing me to her because she wanted to give

herself. It was an expression of love which cannot be expressed with the language of the flesh, nor with the letters of the alphabet." Rene Laurentin and Michel Corteville, *The Discovery of the Secret of La Salette: Official English Translation of the Theotokans* (Holy Water Books, 2023), 95.

[7] Sister Lúcia of Jesus and of the Immaculate Heart, *Fatima in Lucia's Own Words*, ed. Louis Kondor, trans. Dominican Nuns of the Perpetual Rosary (Fatima, Portugal: Secretariado dos Pastorinhos, 1976), 174.

[8] St. Francis de Sales, *Introduction to the Devout Life*, trans. and ed. John K. Ryan (Image Books, 1972), 192.

[9] Each member of the Holy Trinity is uncreated, while each member of a human family is created. The Holy Spirit proceeds from the Father and the Son, but the Holy Spirit is not created by the Father and the Son.

[10] St. Teresa of Calcutta, Nobel Peace Prize acceptance speech, December 10, 1979, University of Oslo, Norway.

[11] Pope Pius XI, Encyclical *Casti Connubii*, December 31, 1930, par. 11.

DAY 12

[1] Servant of God Catherine Doherty, *Grace in Every Season: Through the Year with Catherine Doherty* (Combermere, Canada: Madonna House, 2001), 125.

[2] Sister Lucia dos Santos of Fatima, "Fatima Visionary Predicted 'Final Battle' Would Be Over Marriage, Family," Catholic News Agency, July 8, 2016 In an interview, Cardinal Caffarra recounts that Sister Lucia wrote to him saying: "'The final battle between the Lord and the kingdom of Satan will be about Marriage and the Family.' Don't be afraid, she added [in the letter,] because anyone who works for the sanctity of Marriage and the Family will always be fought and opposed in every way, because this is the decisive issue. Then she concluded: 'Nevertheless, Our Lady has already crushed his head.'"

[3] Though the marriage of Mary and Joseph did not include the conjugal act (sexual intercourse), nor even the intent of it, it was nevertheless a true or real marriage. Our Lady was certainly not,

as some preachers are fond of saying, an "unwed mother." According to St. Thomas Aquinas, Mary and Joseph "consented to the conjugal uniting, but not expressly to the fleshly uniting save on condition that it should please God" (*Summa Theologiae* III, q. 29, a. 2, citing *On Marriage and Concupiscence* I). To further prove that their marriage was a true marriage, St. Thomas Aquinas also quotes from St. Augustine: "All the goods of marriage are fulfilled in these parents of Christ: offspring, fidelity, and sacrament. The offspring we know to have been the Lord Jesus himself; fidelity, because there was no adultery; sacrament, because there was no divorce. Only marital intercourse was not present there."

[4] Sister Lucia dos Santos of Fatima, "Fatima Visionary Predicted 'Final Battle' Would Be Over Marriage, Family."

[5] St. Josemaría Escrivá, *The Way*, chapter "Mortification," par. 174, Escriva.org

[6] G. K. Chesterton, *The Superstition of Divorce* (London: Chatto & Windus, 1920), 73.

[7] St. Josemaría Escrivá, quoted in Scott Hahn, *Ordinary Work, Extraordinary Grace: My Spiritual Journey in Opus Dei* (Image Books, 2006), 102.

[8] St. Teresa of Calcutta, "Mother Teresa: Suffering is the Kiss of Jesus — You've Come So Close that He Can Kiss You" (Commencement Address to the Class of 1982, given at Thomas Aquinas College, Santa Paula, California, June 5, 1982), posted March 3, 2025, by Scott Smith, YouTube, 30 min. 59 sec., https://youtu.be/RC6o0OmQ4sU?si=yEdkdmA13Nxu3RNi.

[9] St. Teresa of Calcutta, *A Simple Path* (Ballantine Books, 1995), 80–81.

[10] Pope John Paul II, General Audience, January 12, 1994, par. 5, translated from the Italian, also cited in Greg Burke, *An Invitation to Joy* (Simon & Schuster, 1999), 111.

DAY 13

[1] Pope Benedict XVI, Angelus message, December 27, 2009.

[2] Ibid.

[3] Ibid.

DAY 14

[1] Luis Laso de la Vega, *The Story of Guadalupe: Luis Laso de la Vega's Nican Mopohua*, trans. Virgilio Elizondo and Timothy Matovina (Rowman & Littlefield, 1997), 79.

DAY 15

[1] Pope John Paul II, Angelus message, December 31, 2000.

[2] Specifically, the Levitical subtribe, the Kohathites, among whom were Abinadab and his sons, Uzzah and Ahio.

[3] There are multiple connections between David's journey described in 2 Samuel 6 and Mary's Visitation of Elizabeth in Luke 1. These include the various locations of the "hill country of Judah" and the close proximity between Uzzah's death and the home of Zechariah and Elizabeth; the fact that both David and Elizabeth, respectively, said of the Ark and Mary, "Who am I that the [Ark/Mother] of my Lord should come to me?" Other similarities include that David and Mary both stayed "three months" in the house of Obededom and Elizabeth, respectively; that David and St. John the Baptist both leapt naked before the Ark; and that both David and Elizabeth "exclaimed" with a loud voice.

[4] Isaiah 53:4, 7: "[Y]et we esteemed him stricken, smitten by God, and afflicted. … He was oppressed, and he was afflicted, yet he opened not his mouth; like a lamb that is led to the slaughter."

DAY 16

[1] Fulton J. Sheen, *Advent and Christmas with Fulton J. Sheen*, ed. Judy Bauer (Liguori Publications, 2001), 7.

[2] Pope John Paul II, Angelus message, December 8, 1998.

[3] Jean-Pierre de Caussade, *Abandonment to Divine Providence* (Exeter: Catholic Records Press, 1921), chapter 2, section 1, 15.

[4] The original word here is "caravansary," plural "caravanserai," which was an inn with a central courtyard for travelers found in the desert regions of Asia or North Africa.

[5] G. K. Chesterton, *The Everlasting Man* (Dodd, Mead and Company, 1925), 45.

[6] Fulton J. Sheen, *Life of Christ* (McGraw-Hill, 1958), 27.

[7] Ibid., 26.

[8] St. Alphonsus Liguori, *The Incarnation, Birth, and Infancy of Jesus Christ*, trans. Eugene Grimm (New York: Benziger Brothers, 1887), 147.

[9] Ibid.

[10] St. Teresa of Calcutta, "Mother Teresa Sends Message of Love, Peace," *Deseret News*, December 23, 1996.

[11] Pope John Paul II, "Midnight Mass Homily," December 24, 2002.

[12] Jean-Pierre de de Caussade, *Abandonment to Divine Providence* (Exeter: Catholic Records Press, 1921), chapter 1, section 2, 11.

[13] It comes from the Hebrew words *bêth* (house) and *lehem* (bread).

[14] Sheen, *Life of Christ*, 27.

DAY 18

[1] G. K. Chesterton, *The Everlasting Man* (Dodd, Mead and Company, 1925), 45.

[2] St. Thérèse of Lisieux, *Story of a Soul: The Autobiography of St. Thérèse of Lisieux*, trans. Thomas N. Taylor (Holy Water Books, 2021), 60–61. The exact quote does not appear, however, in *Story of a Soul*. Instead, we find the following: "Papa had taught me: 'Time is thy barque, and not thy dwelling-place.' Young as I was, these words restored my courage, and even now, in spite of having outgrown many pious impressions of childhood, the symbol of a ship always delights me and helps me to bear the exile of this life. Does not the Wise Man tell us — 'Life is like a ship that passeth through the waves: when it is gone by, the trace thereof cannot be found' (Wisdom 5:10)?"

DAY 19

[1] See also Mt 27:29; Mk 15:18; Jn 19:3.

[2] *Kecharitomene* is the Greek word that translates to "full of grace." It is often mis-translated as "highly favored one," as a kind of diminishment of Mary's unique position in the order of grace.

[3] St. Bernard of Clairvaux, quoted in St. Bonaventure, *Itinerarium Mentis in Deum* [The journey of the mind to God] (St. Athanasius Publishing, 2014), chapter 4, par. 4.

[4] Although the following ranking of the choirs of angels is not official Church dogma, this schema became popular in the Middle Ages in the writings of St. Thomas Aquinas (*Summa Theologiae*, I-I q. 55, a. 3), Dante, St. Hildegard of Bingen, Blessed John Scotus, and Dionysius the Pseudo-Areopagite (C.H., vi, 2 in P.G., III, 200 D).

[5] Fr. William Saunders, "The Devil, the Fallen Angel," Catholic Education Research Center, https://catholiceducation.org/en/culture/the-devil-the-fallen-angel.html. Originally printed in the *Arlington Catholic Herald*, October 19, 2000.

[6] In the original article in the *Arlington Catholic Herald*, Fr. Saunders adds a note here: "These all respond to the intellect of man with virtue as the central rank of angels that determine dominion over the influences of the flesh, the world, and the devil. As will be shown later, the Holy Family Rosary will increase our pondering of the importance for virtues' practice in our lives."

[7] St. Josemaría Escrivá, *Furrow* (Scepter Publishers, 1986), 690.

[8] St. Louis de Montfort, *St. Louis de Montfort's Total Consecration to Jesus through Mary: New, Day-by-Day, Easier-to-Read Translation*, trans. Scott L. Smith, Jr., (Holy Water Books, 2019), 101, also 86.

[9] This requires of us a kind of noble slavery to Mary, in which all our good works, instead of being recorded in our own ledger, are given to Mary.

[10] St. John Vianney, *The Little Catechism of the Curé of Ars* (Tan Books, 1987), xxxiv.

[11] St. Josemaría Escrivá, *Furrow* (Scepter Publishers, 1986), 693.

[12] Pope St. Gregory the Great, *Homilies on the Gospels,* trans. David Hurst, (Cistercian Publications, 1990), Homily 34.

DAY 20

[1] Buddhism had only recently emerged from Hinduism at the time of Christ, and Islam would not appear until hundreds of years after Christ, as a splinter religion from Christianity.

[2] Pope Leo XIII, encyclical *Annum Sacrum*, May 25, 1899, "Form of Consecration to the Most Sacred Heart of Jesus," as prescribed by him on the occasion of the Consecration of the World to the Sacred Heart: "Most Sweet Jesus, Redeemer of the human race … Be you king also of all those who sit in the ancient superstition of

the Gentiles, and refuse not you to deliver them out of darkness into the light and kingdom of God. Grant, O Lord, to your Church, assurance of freedom and immunity from harm; give peace and order to all nations, and make the earth resound from pole to pole with one cry: Praise to the divine heart that wrought our salvation; to it be glory and honor forever. Amen."

[3] Pope John Paul II, Homily, January 6, 1996.

[4] St. John Chrysostom, "Homily VI on Matthew," in *The Homilies of St. John Chrysostom on the Gospel of St. Matthew*, trans. George Prevost and revised by M.B. Riddle, vol. 10 of *Nicene and Post-Nicene Fathers*, ed. Philip Schaff (Hendrickson Publishers, 1994), 45–46.

[5] St. Peter Chrysologus, "Sermon 160," in *The Fathers of the Church: A New Translation*, vol. 17, trans. G. Ganss (Catholic University of America Press, 1953), 217.

[6] Pope Benedict XVI, *Jesus of Nazareth: The Infancy Narratives*, trans. Philip J. Whitmore (Image Books, 2012), 95.

[7] Pope St. Leo the Great, *Nicene and Post-Nicene Fathers*, 2nd ser., vol. 12, trans. Charles Lett Feltoe, (Buffalo, NY: Christian Literature Publishing Co., 1895) sermon 36, part 1.

[8] Ibid.

[9] Ibid.

DAY 21

[1] The *Nunc Dimittis* is part of Compline (also called Night Prayer or Prayers at the End of the Day), which is the final prayer liturgy of the day for the Divine Office (also called the Liturgy of the Hours). The name "Compline" is derived from the Latin word *completorium*, meaning "completion."

[2] Jacopone da Todi, "*Stabat Mater*," trans. Edward Caswall, in *The Roman Missal*, 1962 ed. (Benziger Brothers, 1962). The "*Stabat Mater*" is a 13th-century hymn that is often sung during the Stations of the Cross.

[3] St. Bonaventure, in St. Alphonsus Liguori, *The Glories of Mary* (New York: P.J. Kenedy, 1888), 531.

[4] Ibid.

[5] Ibid.

[6] Ibid.

[7] Ibid.

DAY 22

[1] Fr. Francis L. Filas, SJ, *The Family For Families: Reflections On The Life of Jesus, Mary, and Joseph* (Loyola University Press, 1959), Chapter 7.

[2] St. Pio of Pietrelcina, *Letters*, trans. Geraldine Nolan (San Giovanni Rotondo: Our Lady of Grace Capuchin Friary, 1976), 2:123.

[3] See also Genesis 3, Revelation 12.

[4] St. Francis of Assisi, *The Little Flowers of St. Francis of Assisi*, trans. Raphael Brown (Image Books, 1958), 133.

[5] St. Josemaría Escrivá, *The Way*, trans. Frances Partridge (London: Scepter Publishers, 1982), Point 1, 1.

[6] St. John Chrysostom, *Homilies on the Gospel of John*, in *Nicene and Post-Nicene Fathers,* 1st ser., vol. 14, ed. Philip Schaff (New York: Christian Literature Publishing Co., 1889), Homily 46.

[7] Pope St. Leo the Great, "Sermon 33: On the Feast of the Epiphany," in *Nicene and Post-Nicene Fathers*, 1st ser., vol. 12, ed. Philip Schaff and Henry Wace (New York: Christian Literature Publishing Co., 1895), 133.

[8] See for example *The Gospel of Pseudo-Matthew*, chapter 23: "And it came to pass, when the most blessed Mary went into the temple with the little child, that all the idols prostrated themselves on the ground, so that all of them were lying on their faces shattered and broken to pieces; and thus they plainly showed that they were nothing. Then was fulfilled that which was said by the prophet Isaiah: Behold, the Lord will come upon a swift cloud, and will enter Egypt, and all the handiwork of the Egyptians shall be moved at His presence." *Ante-Nicene Fathers,* vol. 8, trans. Alexander Roberts, Sir James Donaldson, Arthur Cleveland Coxe (1886). See also St. Athanasius, who in his book *On the Incarnation*, discusses the impact of Christ's presence on pagan idols, stating that "at the presence of the true God, all the idols are destroyed." Athanasius, *On the Incarnation*, trans. and ed. John Behr (St. Vladimir's Seminary Press, 2011), 55.

[9] Cornelius à Lapide, *The Great Commentary of Cornelius à Lapide: St. Matthew's Gospel*, trans. Thomas W. Mossman (London: John Hodges, 1889), 2:14.

[10] St. John Chrysostom, quoted in à Lapide, *The Great Commentary of Cornelius à Lapide,* 2:14; see also Trismegistus, quoted by St. Augustine (*City of God*, bk. 8, chap. 14), who says, "Egypt is an image of Heaven, and the temple of the whole world."

DAY 23

[1] St. Teresa of Ávila, *The Interior Castle or the Mansions of St. Teresa of* Ávila*: New Study Guide Edition,* trans. Rev. Benedict Zimmerman, OCD (Holy Water Books, 2024), par. 6, 240.

[2] St. Maria Faustina Kowalska, *The Diary of St. Maria Faustina Kowalska*, (Marian Press, 2020), par. 275, 132.

[3] Ibid., par. 785, 312, italics in original.

[4] St. Teresa of Ávila, *The Book of the Foundations*, trans. Kieran Kavanaugh, OCD, and Otilio Rodriguez, OCD (ICS Publications, 1985), 5.

[5] Pope John Paul II, Homily during Holy Mass in Bellahouston Park, Glasgow, Scotland, June 1, 1982.

[6] St. Teresa of Ávila, *The Way of Perfection*, trans. F. Benedict Zimmerman, OCD (London: Thomas Baker, 1919), chap. 12, 68.

DAY 24

[1] St. Bernard of Clairvaux, *Sermons of St. Bernard on Advent and Christmas Including the Famous Treatise on the Incarnation Called "Missus Est"* (Benziger Brothers, 1909), 31.

[2] Pope John Paul II, Encyclical *Veritatis Splendor*, August 6, 1993, par. 10.

[3] Ibid.

[4] Ibid., par. 12; see also Rom 2:15.

[5] St. Thomas Aquinas, quoted in *Veritatis Splendor*, par. 12.

[6] Ibid., see also Wis 18:4; Ezek 20:41.

[7] St. Augustine, "Sermon 19," in *The Liturgy of the Hours*, vol. 3 (Catholic Book Publishing Corp., 1975), sections 2–3.

[8] It should again be noted that, though the marriage of Mary and Joseph did not include the conjugal act, nor even the intent of one, it was nevertheless a true or real marriage. Our Lady was certainly not, as some preachers are fond of saying, an "unwed mother." According to St. Thomas Aquinas, Mary and Joseph "consented to the conjugal uniting, but not expressly to the fleshly uniting save on condition that it should please God" (*Summa Theologiae III*, q. 29, a. 2, citing *On Marriage and Concupiscence I*). To further prove that their marriage was a true marriage, Aquinas also quotes from St. Augustine: "All the goods of marriage are fulfilled in these parents of Christ: offspring, fidelity, and sacrament. The offspring we know to have been the Lord Jesus himself; fidelity, because there was no adultery; sacrament, because there was no divorce. Only marital intercourse was not present there."

[9] Sister Lucia dos Santos of Fatima, quoted in "Fatima Visionary Predicted 'Final Battle' Would Be Over Marriage, Family," Catholic News Agency, July 8, 2016. In an interview, Cardinal Caffarra recounts that Sister Lucia wrote a letter to him in which she said: "'The final battle between the Lord and the kingdom of Satan will be about Marriage and the Family.' Don't be afraid, she added, [he said,] because whoever works for the sanctity of Marriage and the Family will always be fought and opposed in every way, because this is the decisive issue. Then she concluded: 'Nevertheless, Our Lady has already crushed his head.'"

[10] Pope Leo XIII, *Inscrutabili Dei Consilio* (1878), par. 14. For his part, Leo XIII devoted particular attention to the family throughout his pontificate. In the encyclical letter on socialism, *Quod Apostolici Muneris* (1878), he denounced socialism's insistent interest in destroying marriage as a preliminary to the destruction of society; see also Federico Rodriguez, ed., *Doctrina Pontificia: Documentos Sociales*, vol. 3 (Madrid: Biblioteca de Autores Cristianos, 1969), 172–173, 177, 186–187; as described in *Complete Works of St. José Manyanet*, vol. 4, ed. Joseph M. Blanquet, SF, trans. Scott Smith (Madrid: Biblioteca de Autores Cristianos, 2010), 16.

[11] Pope Leo XIII, Encyclical *Arcanum*, par. 29. *Arcanum* consists of an introduction and three central parts. Part 1 discusses Christian marriage (its origin and properties, ennoblement by Christ, purpose in Christianity, and the power of the Church); part 2 deals with

attacks against it (denial of the power of the Church, attempt to separate contract and marriage, the principles of naturalism, fruits of Christian marriage, evils of divorce, and the attitude of the Church towards divorce); and part 3 provides the remedies to these attacks (civil power and ecclesiastical power, exhortation to bishops, marriages with Catholics). He concludes: "God grant, then, that the greater its importance and gravity, the more docile and ready to obey it, the more docile and ready to obey it will be found everywhere. Let us all implore for this, with fervent prayers, the help of the Blessed Immaculate Virgin Mary, who, inclining men to submit to the faith, will show herself the mother and protector of men." Cited in *Complete Works of St. José Manyanet*, vol. 4, 16.

[12] Sister Lucia dos Santos of Fatima, quoted in "Fatima Visionary Predicted 'Final Battle' Would Be Over Marriage, Family."

DAY 25

[1] Pope John Paul II, Angelus message, December 29, 2002.

[2] See also Pope John Paul II, Angelus message, December 30, 2001.

[3] Pope John Paul II, Angelus message, December 27, 1998.

[4] St. Augustine, *Confessions*, trans. Henry Chadwick (Oxford: Oxford University Press, 1991), bk. III, 6, 11. The Latin original is "*interior intimo meo et superior summo meo*" ("higher than my highest and more inward than my innermost self").

[5] Pope John Paul II, *Gratissimam Sane* (Letter to Families), February 2, 1994, par. 23.

[6] Nazareth comes from the Hebrew word *nazar* (נָזַר) meaning "to consecrate, to separate, to abstain" and the Hebrew word *netser* (נֵצֶר) meaning "branch, shoot, sprout."

[7] Pope Leo XIII, Apostolic Letter *Breve Neminem Fugit*, June 14, 1892.

[8] St. José Manyanet, *Complete Works of St. José Manyanet*, vol. 4, ed. Josep M. Blanquet, SF, trans. Scott Smith (Madrid: Biblioteca de Autores Cristianos, 2010), footnote 55.

[9] Ibid. To give an idea of the routine for family life designed by St. José Manyanet, he wrote pamphlets with the following titles to be given to families: Holy Mass, proposing two ways of hearing

it; communion, with preparation and thanksgiving; two models of points of meditation on the Blessed Sacrament; fruits of communion; spiritual communion; fifteen minutes in the company of Jesus in the Blessed Sacrament; visit to Jesus in the Blessed Sacrament; act of consecration to the Sacred Heart of Jesus; five visits to Jesus in the Blessed Sacrament, etc.; see also Manyanet, *Complete Works of St. José Manyanet*, 370–414.

DAY 26

[1] Pope John Paul II, Angelus message, December 29, 1996.

[2] Pope John Paul II, Angelus message, December 30, 2001.

[3] It should be noted that the Protestants changed the source and numbering of the Ten Commandments in the 16th century from Deuteronomy 5 to Exodus 20, splitting the First Commandment into two and combining the last two into a single commandment.

[4] See also Strong's Lexicon, "honor" as in Dt 5:16; the Hebrew. *kabad* or *kabed* means "to be heavy, to be honored, to be glorified, to be burdensome."

[5] St. Bernard of Clairvaux, *Sermons of St. Bernard on Advent and Christmas: Including the Famous Treatise on the Incarnation Called "Missus Est"* (Benziger Bros, 1909), 31.

[6] Pope St. John Paul II, Letter to Archbishop Pasquale Macchi, August 15, 1993 (Vatican: Tipografia Vaticana, 1993), 16–17. Archbishop Macchi was pontifical delegate for the sanctuary of the Holy House of Loreto on the occasion of the eighth centenary of this sanctuary, which prompted the letter.

[7] Pope St. John Paul II, Angelus message, December 30, 2001.

[8] St. Josemaría Escrivá, *The Way*, trans. Vernon J. Zimmermann (Scepter Publishers, 2006), par. 983.

[9] St. Augustine, *Confessions*, trans. Henry Chadwick (Oxford: Oxford University Press, 1991), bk. I, 1.

DAY 27

[1] Pope Leo XIII, Encyclical *Quamquam Pluries*, August 15, 1889.

[2] Tertullian, *On the Prescription of Heretics*, in *The Liturgy of the Hours*, vol. 2 (Catholic Book Publishing Co., 1976), 1810–12.

[3] St. Ephrem the Syrian, quoted in Rosalie Marie Levy, *Joseph the Just Man* (Daughters of St. Paul, 1955), 152.

[4] St. Teresa of Ávila, quoted in Rosalie Marie Levy, *Joseph the Just Man*, (Daughters of St. Paul, 1955), 146.

[5] St. Francis de Sales, quoted in Francis L. Filas, SJ, *Joseph and Jesus: A Theological Study of Their Relationship* (Bruce Publishing Co., 1952), 99.

DAY 28

[1] Pope John Paul II, Encyclical *Redemptoris Mater*, March 25, 1987, par. 18. He is citing here the Second Vatican Ecumenical Council, *Dogmatic Constitution on Divine Revelation Dei Verbum*, par. 5.

[2] St. Thomas Aquinas, see also ST II-II, Q. 104, Art. 2

[3] St. Thomas Aquinas, ST II-II, Q. 47, Art. 14, ad. 1.

[4] St. Thérèse of Lisieux, *The Story of a Soul*, trans. John Clarke, OCD, and David Clarke, OCD (ICS Publications, 2009), Chapter 9.

[5] Pope John Paul II, *Redemptoris Mater*, par. 4.

[6] Sr. Mary Wilhelmina Lancaster, OSB, "Mrs. Carpenter," unpublished poem provided by Sr. Scholastica of the Abbey of Our Lady of Ephesus of the Benedictines of Mary, Queen of Apostles in Gower, Missouri, for use with this consecration.

[7] Pope Benedict XVI, *From the Depths of Our Hearts: Priesthood, Celibacy, and the Crisis of the Catholic Church*, trans. Michael J. Miller (Ignatius Press, 2020), 137.

[8] Pope John Paul II, *Redemptoris Mater*, par. 20.

[9] Ibid., par. 14.

[10] The original Greek text reads *andra ou ginosko* (ἄνδρα οὐ γινώσκω), which translates literally as "man not I know" or in English "I know not man."

DAY 29

[1] St. Francis de Sales, quoted in *The Catholic Church: The Teacher of Mankind* (Catholic Publication Society Co., 1905), 85.

[2] St. Mary Magdalene de Pazzi, in Placido Fabrini, *The Life and Works of St. Mary Magdalen de-Pazzi*, trans. Antonio Isoleri (Philadelphia: Peter F. Cunningham, 1866), 125.

[3] St. Francis de Sales, *The Spiritual Maxims of St. Francis de Sales*, trans. C. F. Kelley (Benziger Brothers, 1924), 45.

[4] St. Bernard of Clairvaux, quoted in Rosalie Marie Levy, *Joseph the Just Man* (Daughters of St. Paul, 1955), 27–28.

[5] Mother Teresa, quoted by Fr. M. Jeffery Bayhi in interview on December 2024. Fr. Bayhi was the priest who gave Mother Teresa Last Rites and was also a frequent guest in Calcutta during the last decade of her life.

[6] Ven. Aloysius Schwartz, *Poverty: Sign of Our Times* (Society of St. Paul, 1970), 87.

DAY 30

[1] St. Gregory Nazianzen, *Oration 38*, in *Nicene and Post-Nicene Fathers*, 2nd ser., vol. 7, ed. Philip Schaff and Henry Wace, trans. Charles Gordon Browne and James Edward Swallow (New York: Christian Literature Publishing Co., 1894), 345.

[2] St. Augustine, "Sermon 191: On the Nativity of the Lord," in *The Works of Saint Augustine: A Translation for the 21st Century*, part 3, vol. 6, trans. Edmund Hill, ed. John E. Rotelle (New City Press, 1993), 191.1.

[3] St. John of the Cross, *The Spiritual Canticle*, in *The Collected Works of St. John of the Cross*, trans. Kieran Kavanaugh, OCD, and Otilio Rodriguez, OCD (ICS Publications, 1991), 615-616.

[4] St. Maximilian Kolbe, "Final Sketch," February 17, 1941, in *Immaculate Conception and the Holy Spirit: The Marian Teachings of St. Maximilian Kolbe*, trans. Fr. H. M. Manteau-Bonamy, OP (Franciscan Marytown Press, 1977), 61.

[5] St. Louis-Marie Grignion de Montfort, *A Treatise on the True Devotion to the Blessed Virgin*, trans. Frederick William Faber (Marian Press, 2025), par. 55. Saint Bernard of Clairvaux also explains the role of Mary in his "Sermon on the Nativity of the Blessed Virgin Mary," "She is the aqueduct, or channel, through which the graces of God flow to us."

[6] Ibid. par. 1; the original quote is "Since Jesus came into the world through Mary, it is also through her that he must reign in the world."

[7] St. John Eudes, *The Admirable Heart of Mary*, trans. Charles Di Targiani (Refuge of Sinners Publishing, 2013), 45.

[8] Pope Pius XII, quoted in Francis L. Filas, SJ, *St. Joseph & Daily Christian Living* (Macmillan Co., 1959), 196.

[9] St. Lawrence of Brindisi, *Opera Omnia: Feastday Sermons*, trans. Vernon Wagner, OFM Cap (Delhi, India: Media House, 2007), 539.

DAY 31

[1] This is also the verse said on the six beads of the Chaplet of the Holy Face: "Arise, O Lord! and let Thy enemies be scattered, and let them that hate Thee flee from before Thy Face."

[2] Pope Pius XI, Encyclical *Quas Primas*, December 11, 1925, par. 28, 32.

[3] St. Cyril of Alexandria, quoted in Pope Pius XI, *Quas Primas*, par. 13.

[4] Pope Leo XIII, encyclical *Annum Sacrum*, May 25, 1899, par. 3.

[5] Pope Pius XII, Encyclical *Ad Caeli Reginam*, October 11, 1954, par. 47.

[6] Pope Pius XII, *Ad Caeli Reginam*, par. 36, citing [1] *Festum septem dolorum B. Mariae Virg.*, Tractus; [2] St. Anselm, Eadmerus, *De excellentia Virginis Mariae*, c. 11: PL CLIX, 508 A B.

[7] Pope Pius IX, decree *Quemadmodum Deus*, December 8, 1870, par. 5.

[8] A global drought in the 1870s caused mass starvation in South America, Africa, and Asia, leading to the deaths of 50 million people. "It is one of the worst humanitarian disasters in human history," says Deepti Singh at Washington State University, "the most severe event in the 800-year record in Asia." Michael Marshall, "A Freak 1870s Climate Event Caused Drought Across Three Continents," *The New Scientist*, October 30, 2018.

[9] Pope Pius IX, *Quemadmodum Deus*, par. 1, 3.

[10] Ibid.

[11] Ibid., par. 3.

[12] Pope Leo XIII, Apostolic Letter *Breve Neminem Fugit*, June 14, 1892.

DAY 32

[1] St. Alphonsus Liguori, *The Passion and the Death of Jesus Christ*, trans. Eugene Grimm (New York: Benziger Brothers, 1887), 472.

[2] Pope Paul VI, "Address at Nazareth," January 5, 1964, in *The Pope Speaks* 9, no. 1 (1964): 9–10.

[3] Ibid.

[4] Pope Leo XIII, Apostolic Letter *Breve Neminem Fugit*, June 14, 1892.

[5] St. Joan of Arc, quoted in "Famous Quotations by Joan of Arc," Ontario College of Teachers, https://www.code.on.ca/files/assets/resources/88-heroes/documents/ada1o-heroes-blm8famous-quotations.pdf.

[6] St. Ignatius of Antioch, "Epistle to the Romans," in *The Apostolic Fathers*, trans. and ed. Michael W. Holmes, 3rd ed. (Baker Academic, 2007), 175.

[7] St. Thomas More, quoted in *Paris Newsletter*, August 4, 1535 (contemporaneous account), translated in "I Die the King's Good Servant, and God's First," Center for Thomas More Studies.

[8] St. Bernard of Clairvaux, quoted in St. Alphonsus Liguori, *The Glories of Mary* (New York: P.J. Kenedy, 1888).

[9] Ibid.

[10] Ibid.

[11] Ibid.

[12] Fr. Steven Scheier, quoted in Scott L. Smith, *Near Death Experiences* (Sophia Institute Press, 2025), 151.

[13] Ibid., 154.

[14] Blessed Anne Catherine Emmerich, *The Life of Jesus Christ and Biblical Revelations*, trans. "an American Nun," vol. 1 (TAN Books, 1986), 330; see also Rosalie A. Turton, ed., *St. Joseph as Seen by Mystics and Historians* (101 Foundation, Inc., 2000), 344.

[15] St. Alphonsus Liguori, *The Glories Of Mary* (TAN Books, 1968), 102.

[16] Pope Leo XIII, Encyclical *Quamquam Pluries*, August 15, 1889, par. 3.

DAY 33

[1] Concluding prayer of "The Litany of the Holy Family," from the Archconfraternity of the Holy Family.

[2] Pope Leo XIII, Apostolic Letter *Breve Neminem Fugit*, June 14, 1892.

[3] *Complete Works of St. José Manyanet*, ed. Josep M. Blanquet, SF, trans. Scott Smith, vol. 6 (Madrid: Biblioteca de Autores Cristianos, 2010), 1018.

[4] Pope St. John Paul II, Angelus message, December 28, 2003.

[5] St. Ephrem the Syrian, *Sermo de Domino Nostro*, sections 3–4, 9, in *The Liturgy of the Hours*, vol. 2 (Catholic Book Publishing Co., 1976), 735–736.

[6] Pope St. John Paul II, Angelus message, December 28, 2003.

[7] Pope Paul VI, "Address at Nazareth," January 5, 1964.

[8] Pope St. John Paul II, Angelus message, December 29, 2002.

[9] Pope Leo XIII, Apostolic Letter *Breve Neminem Fugit*.

PRAYERS

[1] © Oblates of St. Joseph, Santa Cruz, CA, 1991. Imprimatur with *The Holy Spouses Rosary*, 1st ed., Msgr. Myron Cotta, Diocesan Administrator, Diocese of Fresno, January 23, 2012. Used with permission.

[2] *Complete Works of St. José Manyanet*, ed. Josep M. Blanquet, SF, trans. Scott Smith, vol. 6, (Madrid: Biblioteca de Autores Cristianos, 2010), 658–659.

[3] Ibid., 1018.

About the Authors

Father Donald H. Calloway, MIC, a convert to Catholicism, is a member of the Congregation of Marian Fathers of the Immaculate Conception. Before his conversion, he was a high school dropout who had been kicked out of a foreign country, institutionalized twice, and thrown in jail multiple times. (The story is told in his bestselling memoir, *No Turning Back: A Witness to Mercy*.)

After his radical conversion, Fr. Calloway was ordained to the priesthood in 2003. He earned a BA in philosophy and theology from the Franciscan University of Steubenville, Ohio; MDiv and STB degrees from the Dominican House of Studies in Washington, D.C.; and an STL in Mariology from the International Marian Research Institute in Dayton, Ohio. He currently serves as Vocation Director and Vicar Provincial for the Mother of Mercy Province of the Marian Fathers of the Immaculate Conception of the Blessed Virgin Mary.

Father Calloway leads pilgrimages to Marian shrines around the world and is the author of 22 books with Marian Press, including *Consecration to St. Joseph: The Wonders of Our Spiritual Father* (2020), *Virtues of the Saints: 15 Heavenly Habits for Children* (2025), and *Chaste Heart Gems: Daily Wisdom on the Heart of St. Joseph* (2025). Find out more at FatherCalloway.com.

Scott L. Smith, Jr., is a Louisiana author, attorney, and father of six children. He served as an Assistant Attorney General with the Office of the Louisiana Attorney General from 2015–2019 before entering private practice.

Scott is the co-author with Fr. Donald Calloway, MIC, of *Consecration to St. Joseph for Children & Families* (Marian Press, 2022). He regularly contributes to his Catholic blog (thescottsmithblog.com) and is the co-host of the Catholic Nerds Podcast.

More Inspiration from Fr. Calloway

Virtues of the Saints
15 Heavenly Habits for Children

In this children's book, authors Patrick O'Hearn and Fr. Donald Calloway, MIC, with beautiful illustrations by Adalee Hude, describe 15 of the most important virtues for boys and girls. We begin by defining the virtue, followed by an example showing how one saint, from Our Lady and St. Joseph to St. Kateri Tekawitha and St. Carlo Acutis, and more, lived out that virtue. Hardcover with dustjacket. 86 pages. **Y134-VIRT**

The Chaste Heart of St. Joseph
A Graphic Novel

How much do you really know about St. Joseph? He was once a little boy and played like all children. He had royal blood, and could have been a king. He was a young man when he married Mary. He was a wonderful father to Jesus. He was the brave and steadfast protector of the Holy Family. He's the model of manhood. He's worked many miracles and is a powerful intercessor for us … and he had a pure, chaste heart. In this colorful graphic novel for children of all ages, Fr. Donald Calloway tells the dynamic and inspiring story of St. Joseph, our spiritual father and the "Terror of Demons." You'll learn that, whenever you need help, just "Go to Joseph!" Hardcover. 84 pages. **Y134-JOEG**

The Litany of St. Joseph
Coloring Book

Color, learn, pray! Father Donald Calloway, MIC, presents a fun way for children of all ages to grow closer to St. Joseph, the ultimate superhero and the "Terror of Demons." Learn more about this great Saint by coloring the wonderful illustrations by Sam Estrada, each portraying a different title of St. Joseph. 36 pages. **Y134-JCOBK**

No Turning Back:
A Witness to Mercy

In this new edition, Fr. Donald Calloway looks back in a new introduction to this perennially powerful witness to the transforming grace of God and the Blessed Mother's love for her children. His witness proves a key truth of our faith: Between Jesus, the Divine Mercy, and Mary, the Mother of Mercy, there's no reason to give up hope on anyone, no matter how far they are from God. Paperback. 288 pages. Includes photo section. **Y134-ANTBK**

Call 1-800-462-7426 or visit FatherCalloway.com